THE

PLAY
OF
WORDS

*Fun and Games
for Language Lovers*

Christmas 1993

Dear Charles,

*Hopefully this book will
provide you with a few
minutes of amusement.*

Happy Holidays!

Love
Holly

Books by Richard Lederer

The Play of Words
Crazy English
Get Thee to a Punnery
Anguished English

THE
PLAY
OF
WORDS

*Fun and Games
for Language Lovers*

Richard Lederer

Illustrations by Bernie Cootner

POCKET BOOKS
New York   London   Toronto   Sydney   Tokyo   Singapore

POCKET BOOKS, a division of Simon & Schuster Inc.
1230 Avenue of the Americas, New York, NY 10020

Copyright © 1990 by Richard Lederer
Illustrations copyright © 1990 Bernie Cootner

ISBN: 0-671-68908-8

First Pocket Books hardcover printing October 1990

10 9 8 7 6 5 4 3 2 1

Design: Stanley S. Drate / Folio Graphics Co. Inc.

To all the games people in my life—
my tennis buddies,
my card buddies,
and my word buddies

CONTENTS

· II ·
CLICHÉS
——

· III ·
SOUND
——

· IV ·
NAMES

—

· V ·
DICTION

—

· VI ·
LOGIC

—

INTRODUCTION

Do you know the connection between the expression *a harrowing experience* and agriculture, between *by and large* and sailing, between *get your goat* and horses, or between *steal your thunder* and show business? You probably have heard the comparisons *happy as a clam, smart as a whip, pleased as punch,* and *dead as a doornail*—but have you ever wondered why a clam should be happy, a whip smart, punch pleased, or a doornail dead?

By playing the fifty games in this book, you'll discover the answers to these questions as well as hundreds of other semantic delights that repose in our marvelous English language. I won't make you comb through scabrous thickets of jumbled letters to extract hidden words just for the sake of passing time. Instead, you'll learn a lot from these mind-opening games—and have a lot of fun learning. During my nearly three decades as a high school English teacher I have found that enjoyment and instruction are inspiring team teachers.

Any games book worth its salt (another phrase that you will find in the pages that follow) contains challenges of varying degrees of difficulty. *The Play of Words* is arranged to provide you with a varied and vigorous regimen of calisthenics for the mind. Some of the questions you will be able to answer right away; others, by design, are impossible for all but the most pyrotechnic of geniuses.

In many cases, a poser may stump you the first time around, but insights will come to you in sudden flashes as you return to the game a second or third time. When you are sure that you have reached your limit, turn to the answers, which appear conveniently at the end of each section.

You can play all the games within a period of a week or two or string them out, one a week, over the course of nearly a year. You can play them solo or in groups or teams. The rules to each game are simple, and you need no more costly equipment than pencil and paper. You may write directly in this book, or you may want to keep these pages pristine and free of hints, so as to share these linguistic adventures with your family and friends.

I thank my publishers for their suggestion that I create a book of word games and my editor, Stacy Schiff, for the loving care with which she helped to make the material clear, correct, and attractive. Versions of some of the games in this book have appeared in *Writing!*, *Words Ways*, and *Verbatim*.

RICHARD LEDERER
Concord, New Hampshire

I

METAPHORS

"Language is fossil poetry which is constantly being worked over for the uses of speech. Our commonest words are worn-out metaphors."

—JAMES BRADSTREET GREENOUGH
AND GEORGE LYMAN KITTREDGE

♦ Body Language

Engaging in mental games is as beneficial to the mind as physical exercise is to the body. Various studies show that playing chess, solving crossword puzzles, and grappling with logic problems energize the brain and can even elevate the I.Q.

As you have opened this book and are reading this page, you are clearly a nimble-witted person who craves exercise for your verbal muscles, sensing that such activity will hone your intelligence. It seems appropriate, then, that before you read the next paragraph, you take a few minutes to write down all the adjectives you can think of to describe someone who is very intelligent.

Chances are that among your answers are words like:

bright	*acute*
brilliant	*clever*
dazzling	*incisive*
lucid	*keen*
scintillating	*sharp*

If you carefully examine these two lists of adjectives, you will notice that each clusters around a single basic concept. All the words on the left compare intelligence to light, including *scintillating,* which descends from the Latin *scintilla,* meaning "spark," and all the words on the right compare intelligence to the edge of a knife, including *clever,* which can be traced directly back to the Old English *cleave* and *cleaver.*

3

Such comparisons are called metaphors. A metaphor (the word originally meant "carry beyond") is a figure of speech that merges two objects or ideas that are, for the most part, different from each other but turn out to be alike in some significant way. We usually think of metaphors as figurative devices that only poets create, but, in fact, all of us make metaphors during almost every moment of our waking lives. As T. E. Hulme has proclaimed, "Prose is a museum where all the old weapons of poetry are kept."

Now think of the tag phrases we use to identify loopy, wiggy, or wifty people who are short on intelligence, judgment, or sanity. Here again English speakers press into service a battalion of figurative comparisons:

light metaphors: he's rather dim; the light's on, but nobody's home;

food metaphors: she's a few cookies short of a dozen, his pail is empty, her kernel never popped, he's a couple of cans short of a six-pack, the butter slipped off her noodle, he's two sandwiches short of a picnic, she's not cooking on all burners, there aren't any beans in his pod, she's one doughnut shy of a dozen, he puts mustard on his Froot Loops, somebody blew out her pilot light;

nautical metaphors: he doesn't have both oars in the water; her line's in the water, but the bait's missing; she hasn't packed a full seabag;

car metaphors: his brain is stuck in first gear, her tank is low, his motor isn't hitting on all cylinders, her battery is dead, he's running on empty, she's driving in reverse, she's got one wheel in the sand;

building-trade metaphors: it's a nice house, but nobody's home; his elevator doesn't go all the way to the top; she's one brick short of a full load; he has a few screws loose; her vacancy sign is always on; the top rung of his ladder is missing; she's a tad off of plumb; he has a room for rent; she's off her hinges; he has a leak in the think tank; her fence doesn't have all its pickets; there are termites in his attic.

Metaphors are a way of explaining the abstract in terms of the concrete. Small wonder that we take our most common metaphors from things that surround us in our daily lives and that we find a rich vein of descriptive phrases in the most familiar of all the things in our lives— our own bodies.

Whether you're a high- or a lowbrow, here's some knee-slapping good fun that you can really sink your teeth into. Try your hand at getting a leg up on some head-to-toe body language. Complete each of the following phrases by using an anatomical part listed below, as in "rule of *thumb*" and *"tongue* in *cheek."* For the record, we get *rule of thumb,* "a rough measure or guideline," from the days when rulers (of the measuring kind) were uncommon and people used the length of the thumb from the knuckle to the tip as an approximate measure of one inch. If you speak literally tongue in cheek, people will have a hard time understanding you. The phrase descends from the old custom of puffing the cheek out with the tongue to indicate that something facetious or insincere has been said:

♦
ANATOMICAL PARTS
♦

- arm
- artery
- back
- belly
- body
- bone
- brain
- breast
- brow
- cheek
- chest
- chin
- craw
- ear
- elbow
- eye
- face
- finger
- flesh
- foot
- gut
- hand
- hair
- head
- heart
- heel
- intestine
- knee
- knuckle
- leg
- limb
- lip
- liver
- lung
- mouth
- nail
- neck
- nose
- rib
- scalp
- shoulder
- skeleton
- spine
- spleen
- stomach
- throat
- thumb
- toe
- tongue
- tooth
- whisker

1. _____ of a needle

2. _____ of contention

3. _____ of the matter

4. _____ of lettuce

5. _____ of a river

6. _____ of a journey

7. _____ of a shoe

8. _____ of an essay

9. that _____ of the woods

10. a _____nail sketch

11. vent one's _____

12. _____-tickling

13. wet behind the _____s

head of lettuce

14. get it off your _____

15. give the cold _____

16. take it on the _____

17. _____ reaction

18. _____–jerk reaction

19. _____ grease

20. _____ service

21. _____ the bill

22. _____ the line

23. _____ under

24. _____ in the closet

25. make a clean _____ of things

26. a cut _____

27. a main _____ of traffic

28. to turn up your _____ at

29. get off my _____

30. fighting _____ and _____

31. yell at the top of your _____s

32. to split _____s

33. _____al fortitude

34. to _____beat

35. a back_____ed compliment

36. sticks in your _____

37. tear _____ from _____

38. turn the other _____

39. have no _____ for

40. _____pots

41. safe by a _____

42. _____storm

43. save _____

44. kick up your _____s

45. up in _____s

46. put the _____ on

47. lily-_____ed

48. _____less coward

49. a _____ laugh

50. a ticket _____er

(Answers on page 70)

♦ HEARTFELT WORDS

In the English language, the heart is often used to denote the seat of passion, compassion, courage, and intelligence. Of all the parts of the body, the heart is the one that throbs most pervasively through our daily conversation. If, for example, we are deeply saddened, we might say that we are *heartsick, heartbroken, downhearted, heavy-hearted,* or *discouraged.* At the heart of *discouraged* beats the Latin *cor,* "heart," giving the word the literal meaning of "disheartened." Or if we wish to emphasize our sincerity, we might say *heartfelt, with all my heart, from the bottom of my heart,* or *in my heart of hearts.*

If something pleases us greatly, we might drag out *heart's delight* or *it warms the cockles of my heart.* The latter is a somewhat redundant statement; a cockle is a bivalve mollusk of the genus *cardium* (Latin "heart") that takes its name from its shape, which resembles that of a human heart.

It was once the custom for a young man to attach to his sleeve a gift for his sweetheart or to wear her name embroidered on his sleeve, thus displaying his feelings for the world to see. Seizing on this practice, Shakespeare gave the world the expression *to wear one's heart on one's sleeve,* meaning "to show one's emotions." In *Othello,* Iago says: "For when my outward action doth demonstrate/The native act and figure of my heart/In compliment extern, 'tis not long after/But I will wear my heart upon my sleeve."

Using the definitions that follow, identify each common word and expression that contains the word *heart:*

heart on a sleeve

1. to take seriously
2. please be merciful
3. beloved person
4. be reassured
5. to desire earnestly
6. to be frightened
7. discouraged
8. incomplete, as in an effort
9. complete, as in an effort
10. substantial, as a meal
11. mental anguish
12. the central issue
13. brave, courageous
14. uninvolved emotionally
15. to be well intentioned
16. to swear to be telling the truth
17. characterizing a good person
18. characterizing a cruel person
19. entertainment idol
20. to give up
21. to regret deeply and painfully
22. one who shows extravagant sympathy
23. to memorize
24. indigestion
25. to play hard
26. just what I like
27. a change of mind
28. to reassure
29. the essential emotion, as of a nation
30. youthful in attitude
31. to be completely frightened
32. characterizing an intimate conversation
33. thoroughly evil
34. cheerful, free from anxiety
35. suspenseful

(Answers on page 70)

◆ CLOTHES MAKE THE LANGUAGE

Next to our bodies, the closest thing to us in our daily lives is our clothing, which is indeed next to our bodies. No surprise then that we have woven so many descriptive phrases from the whole cloth and other materials that we wrap around ourselves. "For the apparel oft proclaims the man," advises Polonius in his famous advice to his son Laertes in *Hamlet*. As you are about to see, the apparel oft proclaims the language, too.

Some of the items of clothing in which our English language is dressed are quite subtle. The word *tire,* for example, is a clipping of *attire*—a "dressing" of rubber on the rim of a wheel. To be *slipshod* originally meant "to be shod in loose-fitting slippers," a slovenly habit of sixteenth-century ne'er-do-wells. The first fettles were girdles that warriors wore around the waist for battle. To be *in fine fettle* meant to be well girded up and ready for action. In modern parlance the phrase has taken on a more abstract meaning, "to be in high spirits."

By now you must be ready to try a new game on for size. Don your thinking cap, keep the news under your hat, keep your shirt on, and try not to come apart at the seams. Complete each common word or expression with an article selected from the following clothes closet:

♦

THE WARDROBE

♦

- apron
- belt
- bonnet
- boot
- bootstraps
- britches
- button
- buttonhole
- cap
- cloak
- clothing
- coat

- coattails
- collar
- cuff
- glove
- gown
- hairpin
- hat
- hood
- jacket
- jock
- necktie
- nightcap

- pajamas
- pants
- pocket
- shirt
- shoe
- shoestring
- sleeve
- stocking
- veil
- vest
- wig

1. to have something up your _____
2. hot under the _____
3. cute as a _____
4. too big for his _____
5. a turn_____
6. a _____legger
7. to be _____winked
8. a stuffed _____
9. tied to his mother's _____ strings
10. a yellow _____
11. town and _____
12. a wolf in sheep's _____
13. to play it close to the _____

too big for his britches

14. a big_____

15. a bee in her _____

16. _____ and dagger

17. a feather in one's _____

18. pick_____

19. a _____ turn

20. to un_____ a new idea

21. a _____ party

22. fits like a _____

23. an off-the-_____ remark

24. the cat's _____

25. goody two-_____s

26. to wear the _____ in the family

27. to fake an opponent out of his _____

28. a blue_____

29. living on a _____

30. to hit below the _____

31. to ride into office on the President's

_____

32. to pull oneself up by one's _____

33. That's not a new idea. It's old _____.

34. to _____ a potential donor

35. Before we go, let's have a _____.

(Answers on page 71)

♦ ## HOUSEHOLD WORDS

Metaphors furnished with common household objects are figures of speech that we literally live with every day. Some of these comparisons are new, such as a *couch potato,* a phrase that compares lumpish watchers of television to lumpy potatoes: the longer couch potatoes sit, the deeper they put down their roots. But most of these turns of phrase are quite old, including *dead as a doornail,* which has been wheezed for more than six hundred years. In 1350 an anonymous poet, describing the hunting of a deer, wrote: "And happened that I hitt him be-hynde the left sholdire./Ded as a dorenail was he fallen." A doornail was a large-headed nail or bolt with which long-ago carpenters studded doors to strengthen and decorate them. The *dead* in the expression *dead as a doornail* means "rigid, immovable," as in *deadline.* When the point of the nail came through the far end, the workmen would bend it over so that it would hold fast. The doornail was then "dead"; that is, it could no longer be removed.

Rather than keeping you on pins and needles any longer, I'll take this game off the back burner. Empty out your kitchen drawer, toolbox, and linen closet to complete fifty expressions out of house and home:

a couch potato

_____◆_____

WORDS CLOSE TO HOME

_____◆_____

- *armchair*
- *barrel*
- *basket*
- *bed*
- *blanket*
- *board*
- *book*
- *bucket*
- *button*
- *can*
- *candle*
- *carpet*
- *chair*
- *clock*
- *comb*
- *cradle*
- *curtain*

- *dish*
- *doormat*
- *drawer*
- *hammer*
- *iron*
- *kettle*
- *key*
- *kitchen sink*
- *light*
- *monkey wrench*
- *mousetrap*
- *nail*
- *pan*
- *picture*
- *pot*
- *purse*
- *putty*

- *razor*
- *rocker*
- *rug*
- *sandpaper*
- *saucer*
- *saw*
- *screwdriver*
- *sheet*
- *sieve*
- *snuff*
- *soap*
- *spoon*
- *stool*
- *table*
- *tack*
- *wringer*

1. _____ pigeon
2. _____ opera
3. off your _____
4. a wet _____
5. a flying _____
6. the iron _____ countries
7. a _____ case
8. a _____ belly
9. the _____'s edge

10. a memory like a _____

11. strange _____fellows

12. a fine _____ of fish

13. out of the frying _____ and into the fire

14. to have someone over a _____

15. the red-_____ treatment

16. _____ quarterback

17. born with a silver _____ in his mouth

18. from the _____ to the grave

19. not up to _____

20. _____man of the board

21. to kick the _____

22. to go over with a fine-tooth _____

23. to throw everything in but the _____

24. to throw the _____ at

25. to burn the _____ at both ends

26. to turn the _____s

27. to _____ out our differences

28. to _____ out an agreement

29. to get down to brass _____s

30. to be put through the _____

31. to open up a _____ of worms

32. lie like a _____

33. out like a ——————————

34. cute as a ——————————

35. pretty as a ——————————

36. rough as ——————————

37. stiff as a ——————————

38. white as a ——————————

39. hits the —————————— on the head

40. I'm just —————————— in your hands.

41. It's first class; it's top ——————————.

42. You can —————————— it out, but you
    can't take it.

43. Vodka and orange juice served with ice is
    called a ——————————.

44. Build a better ——————————, and the
    world will beat a path to your door.

45. She cleaned his ——————————.

46. Hard work is the —————————— to
    success.

47. You can't make a silk ——————————
    out of a sow's ear.

48. A time-honored adage is sometimes called
    an old ——————————.

49. The bad weather threw a ——————————
    into our plans for the picnic.

50. The last place team was the ——————————
    of the league.

(Answers on page 71)

♦ COLORFUL ENGLISH

Colors color our language—and that is not just a pigment of my imagination. Think of the words we use to describe how we feel. At various times we are green with envy, gray with exhaustion, red with embarrassment, or white with rage. We can fall into a black mood, a purple passion, or a blue funk; when things start looking up, we feel in the pink.

Even the animal world gets painted by the coloring of human imagination.

Have you ever owned a white elephant? Before you shake your head no, remember that nowadays the expression *white elephant* means an object of some worth that nobody else seems to want, like a huge out-of-style couch or a pedal-driven sewing machine. *White elephant* refers back to the albino elephants once considered sacred in Siam (now Thailand). These creatures were so rare that each one born became automatically the property of the king and was not permitted to work. When a subject incurred the king's displeasure, the angry monarch would bestow one of his white elephants on him as a gift. The enormous appetite and utter uselessness of the animal would soon plunge the "gifted" man into financial ruin.

The tale and the other etymological treatises in this book are anything but red herrings. The original red herrings were strong-smelling fish that the fox hunters of Old England dragged across the fox's trail to confuse the hounds and give the quarry a sporting chance. Today the meaning of *red herring* has been broadened to signify a misleading statement that diverts our attention from the real issues.

a white elephant

Here's a golden opportunity for you to show your true colors by ranging over the rainbow coalition of hues that color many everyday expressions. In the colorful quiz that follows, complete each phrase with a color. Most of the colors will appear more than once.

Good luck. I'm confident that you'll pass this test with flying colors:

---♦---

THE SPECTRUM

---♦---

- *black*
- *blue*
- *brown*
- *gold*
- *gray*

- *green*
- *lime*
- *pink*
- *purple*
- *red*

- *rose*
- *silver*
- *white*
- *yellow*

1. _____mail
2. a bolt from the _____
3. a _____horn
4. a _____-bellied coward
5. _____grass music
6. good as _____
7. true _____
8. a _____ eminence
9. once in a _____ moon
10. the _____-carpet treatment
11. singing the _____s
12. caught _____-handed

13. _____ prose

14. Every cloud has a _____ lining.

15. For dessert I had an ice-cream-covered
    _____ie.

16. _____ tape

17. He looks at the world through
    _____-colored glasses.

18. The star loves always being in the
    _____-light.

19. beaten _____ and
    _____

20. People who hallucinate are said to see
    _____ elephants.

21. The committee gave her proposal the
    _____ light.

22. _____en oldies

23. the _____ sheep of the family

24. a _____-letter day

25. _____blood

26. a _____ thumb

27. a _____neck

28. a _____guard

29. paint the town _____

30. talking a _____ streak

31. Silence is _____en.

32. to _____wash the truth

33. to _____-bag it

34. Off-color jokes are called _____
    jokes.
35. _____ie points
36. _____ journalism
37. When a business makes a profit, it is in the
    _____.
38. When a business loses money, it is in the
    _____.
39. Mary is a genius. She obviously has lots of
    _____ matter.
40. A woman with intellectual or literary
    interests is called a _____ stocking.
41. a _____ cent
42. _____ as grass
43. Evil magic is _____ magic.
44. Good magic is _____ magic.
45. The boss is so angry that she's seeing
    _____.
46. _____ laws
47. _____-chip stocks
48. a _____ area
49. a _____shoe law firm
50. I hope you're tickled _____ by
    how well you've answered these questions.

Now try this: List at least ten words that describe
both a color and a thing. *Orange* is the best-known example.

(Answers on page 72)

◆ DOWN-TO-EARTH METAPHORS

We were once a nation of farmers, but by the turn of the century most of us had moved to towns and cities. Today only two percent of Americans live on farms, and we have largely lost touch with our agricultural roots. In "God's Grandeur" (1877), the English poet Gerard Manley Hopkins lamented the effects of the Industrial Age on our feeling for the land:

> *And all is seared with trade; bleared, smeared with toil,*
> *And wears man's smudge and shares man's smell: the soil*
> *Is bare now, nor can foot feel, being shod.*

Because our shod (shoed) feet no longer touch the soil, most Americans are unaware of the metaphors that spring from the earth and those who work it. These verbal seeds lie buried so deeply in the humus of our language that we are hardly aware they are figures of speech at all. Let's do some digging to uncover the rich, earthy metaphors from which grow so much of our speech and our writing, our thoughts and our dreaming.

We may be aware of the agricultural comparisons in expressions like *cream of the crop, to crop up, to feel one's oats, to farm out, a farm team, to weed out, to plow into, a vintage year, a grass roots campaign, a budding movie star, easy pickings, gone to seed, seedy, to reap the benefits, cut and dried, to mow down, separate the wheat from the chaff, to cut a wide swath, a needle in a haystack,* and *take your cotton-pickin' hands off my lunch bag!* But most city dwellers have lost contact with the down-to-earth figures of speech embedded in our language.

From the clues provided, unearth each word or phrase:

1. The lines in a worried forehead resemble the grooves in the earth made by a plow. We describe such a forehead as _____.

2. Like well-farmed land, the fertile mind of an intellectual woman or man is carefully tended and yields a bountiful harvest. We say that such people are

_____.

3. Among farm equipment is a cultivating implement set with spikes or spring teeth that pulverizes the earth by violently tearing and flipping over the topsoil. That's why we identify an emotionally lacerating experience as

_____.

4. Rooted in the Latin *de-,* "from," and *lira,* "furrow," is a word that metaphorically compares behavior that deviates from a straight course to the action of swerving from the conventional path in plowing: _____.

5. In bygone days, the Old English *math* meant "mowing." Nowadays a word that means "results, effects, or consequences" is _____.

6. European peasants, forbidden to cut down or pick from trees, were allowed to gather gratuitous fuel and food blown down by acts of nature, a bounty that required little effort on the part of the lucky recipients. By extension, we today use a word that describes an unexpected stroke of good luck: _____.

7. The arduous job of hoeing long rows in uncooperative terrain gives us this American expression that means "a difficult task": _____.

8. Late spring frosts or pests of the insect or human variety can kill an aborning tree or flower before it has a chance to develop. When we terminate a project in its early stages, we say that we _____.

9. Hay is made by setting mown grass out in the sun

a furrowed brow

to dry. When we want to make the most of an opportunity, we try to _____ .

10. Anyone who has ever tried to use tightly stretched wire to bind bales of hay knows how inefficient and ornery the stuff can be. When someone or something behaves in an uncontrolled manner, we say that he, she, or it _____ .

(Answers on page 72)

◆ SEAWORTHY METAPHORS

In "Sea Fever" (1902) the poet John Masefield sang:

> I must go down to the seas again
> To the lonely sea and the sky.
> And all I ask is a tall ship
> And a star to steer her by.

Relatively few of us go down to the seas anymore, and even fewer of us get to steer a tall ship. Having lost our intimacy with the sea and with sailing, we no longer taste the salty flavor of the metaphors that ebb and flow through our language.

Consider our use of the word *ship*. We continue to ship goods, even when that shipping is done by truck, train, or plane. We compliment someone on "running a tight ship," even when that "ship" is an office or a classroom. And many things besides ships can be ship-shape or sinking ships.

Consider, too, our use of the compound word *bailout*. When we talk about a Chrysler or a savings and loan bailout, we are unconsciously comparing a financial strategy to the act of removing water from a sinking craft.

The lapping of the sea at our language is not a difficult concept to fathom. When we try to *fathom* an idea, we are making poetic use of an old word that originally meant "the span between two outstretched arms." Then the word came to mean "a unit of six feet used for measuring the depth of water." By poetic extension, the verb *to fathom* now means "to get to the bottom of" something, and that something doesn't have to be the ocean.

To help you learn the ropes and get your bearings with seafaring metaphors, take a turn at the helm. The coast is clear for you to sound out the lay of the land by taking a different tack and playing a landmark game. Don't go overboard by barging ahead, come hell or high water. If you feel all washed up, on the rocks, in over your head, and sinking fast in a wave of confusion, try to stay on an even keel. As your friendly anchorman, I won't rock the boat by lowering the boom on you.

Now that you get my drift, consider how the following idioms of sailing and the sea sprinkle salt on our tongues: *shape up or ship out, to take the wind out of his sails, the tide turns, a sea of faces, down the hatch, hit the deck, to steer clear of, don't rock the boat, to harbor a grudge,* and *to give a wide berth to.* For ancient mariner, *by and large* was a command that meant "to sail slightly off the wind," in contrast to "full and by." When we say *by and large* today, we mean "in general; for the most part" because we do not wish to sail directly into the topic. The expression *taken aback* probably conjures up in your mind an image of a person caught off guard and staggering backwards. But the origin of the phrase is nautical, too: Sailing *by and large* left an inexperienced helmsman in less danger of being *taken aback,* which meant "to catch the wind on the wrong side of the sails."

Using the clues provided, identify each seaworthy word or phrase:

1. From the Greek word for "ship," we inherit a word that means "illness" but that originally signified "seasickness." That word is _____.

2. The long, narrow central hall of a cruciform church gets it name from *navis,* the Latin word for "ship," because the church is thought of as an ark for its congregants. Many of these long corridors do indeed resemble upside-down ships, and ships are often built bottoms up. These corridors are called _____.

3. The lee is the side of the ship sheltered from the wind. Hence, when we make things easy for others, we give them _____.

4. On sailing ships of yesteryear the "butt" was a popular term for the large, lidded casks that held drinking water. These butts were equipped with "scuttles," openings through which sailors ladled out the water. Just as today's office workers gather about a water cooler to exchange chitchat and rumor, crewmen stood about the scuttled butts to trade _____.

5. The phrase that old salts used to describe a ship in shallow water that touches bottom from time to time has been extended to designate any precarious situation: _____.

6. A much worse situation is one in which a ship strikes bottom and is held tight, unable to proceed. Today we use this expression to identify any rigid rule or opinion: _____.

7. The doldrums are those parts of the ocean near the equator that are noted for calm and neutral weather. They pose no difficulty for fuel-driven vessels, but for sailing ships they mean a dead standstill. When we are stuck in boredom or depression, we are _____.

8. Like a vessel driven ashore beyond the normal high-water mark, one who is abandoned or rejected is _____.

9. Ships' colors used to be raised and lowered a peg at a time. The higher the colors, the greater the honor. Nowadays, we diminish others' self-esteem by _____.

10. In sailing parlance "devil" is not he of the forked tail but a nautical term for the seam between two planks in the hull of a ship, on or below the water line. Anyone who had to caulk such a "devil" was figuratively caught between a rock and a hard place, or between

_____.

11. For sailors, "sheets" refer to the lines attached to the lower corner of a sail. When all three sheets of an old sailing vessel were allowed to run free, they were said to be "in the wind," and the ship would lurch and stagger. That's why we call an unsteady state of drunkenness

_____.

12. Seafaring folk called that part of the cable that is to the rear of the windlass "bitts," and the turn of the cable around the bitts the "bitter." When a ship rides out a gale, the cable is let out to just the place that this game has reached: _____.

(Answers on page 72)

◆ WEATHER OR NOT

You have just seen how our language is rooted in the land and sails on the sea. Now let's explore how English floats in the air and looks up at the heavens.

In an astronomical number of ways our language sees stars. The word *disaster*, for example, comes from the Latin prefix *dis-*, "bad," and root *astrum*, "star"; one who is the victim of a disaster is indeed "ill starred." Have you ever been curious about why the words *lunatic* and *lunar* begin with the same four letters? Once again the study of heavenly etymology supplies us with the answer. *Lunatic* is a reflection of the Latin *luna*, "moon," and is fossil evidence that our forebears believed that prolonged exposure to the light of the moon renders one daft and insane, that is, moonstruck or loony.

For a breath of fresh air, let's move closer to *terra firma*. You probably think about the weather almost every day, but have you ever noticed how much our speech is literally and figuratively under the weather? Certain people strike us as stuffy, chilly, cool, cold, icy, or frigid, while others seem to radiate a warm and sunny disposition. Because temperature, moisture, and wind conditions are so important in our lives, a variety of weather patterns blow hot and cold through many of the descriptive phrases in our speech and writing.

The content of this chapter may make you feel *under the weather*, a common expression that comes to us from the language of sailors. On the high seas when the wind starts to blow hard and the water becomes rough, crewmen and travelers go belowdecks and down to their cabins in order to ride out the storm and avoid becoming seasick. In this way they literally retreat to a location "under the weather."

Now that you're getting acclimated to the concept of weather metaphors, complete each phrase with a pattern from the following chart:

---♦---

THE WEATHER CHART

---♦---

- bolt
- breeze
- climate
- cool
- cloud
- flood
- fog
- frozen

- gale
- hazy
- heat
- ice
- lightning
- misty
- rain
- shower

- slush
- snow
- storm
- sunny
- tempest
- thunder
- whirlwind
- wind

1. _____s of laughter

2. _____ in a teapot

3. steal someone's _____

4. greased _____

5. _____-side up

6. a _____ from the blue

7. a _____ fund

8. a _____ job

9. a _____ tour

10. a _____ of applicants

11. _____ assets

12. shoot the _____

13. brain_____

14. break the _____

15. get _____ of

16. take a _____ check

17. my memory of the evening is _____

18. I'm in a _____

19. on _____ nine

on cloud nine

20. the _____'s on
21. _____ with praise
22. a _____ cat
23. become _____-eyed
24. the _____ of opinion

(Answers on page 72)

◆ **BEASTLY ENGLISH**

We often refer to our fellow organisms who run and fly and swim and creep across the face of our planet as "dumb animals." It is true that these creatures do not speak in the human sense of that word, but they have made thousands of contributions to the power of human speech. Some of our wildlife words and expressions involve the simple transfer of a marked animal characteristic to human activity, such as *eagle-eyed* and *pigheaded*. Others are harder to capture.

The verb *to ostracize*, for example, means "to exclude from a group by popular consent," and hidden in that verb is an oyster. Rather than clamming up and floundering, let's go fishing for the origin of *ostracize*. Oysters were a staple of the ancient Greek diet, and the verb *to ostracize* descends directly from *ostrakon*, the Greek word for an oyster shell. In ancient Athens a citizen could be banished by popular vote of other citizens, who gathered in the marketplace and wrote down the name of the undesirable on a tile or potsherd. If enough votes were dropped into an urn, the victim was sent from the city for five or ten years. Because the shards of pottery resembled oyster shells, they were called *ostrakon*, whence our verb for general exclusion.

Ostracize is but one beastly example of how the creatures who fill the land, sea, and air also fill up our language. In *pecuniary* and *muscle* lurk bulls and mice. *Pecu* is the Latin word for cattle. Because wealth in ancient times was measured in heads of livestock, early metal coins were stamped with the head of a bull. From this

time-honored association between cattle and money we
have gained such words as *pecuniary* and *impecunious*. As
for *muscle*, it is easy to see why the term derives from the
Latin word *musculus*—for "little mouse."

Another category of zoological English is the trans-
mutation of animal nouns into common verbs without
any basic change in form. Because people like to compare
themselves and others to fauna, many animal names have
become verbs that describe human behavior. Choosing
from the exhibit below, identify each beastly verb, as in
"to take more than one deserves: to *hog*":

♦

THE MENAGERIE

♦

- ape
- badger
- bird
- bird dog
- bitch
- buck
- buffalo
- bug
- bull
- carp
- chicken
- clam
- cow
- crab
- crane
- crow
- dog
- duck
- eagle
- fawn
- ferret
- fish
- flounder
- fox
- frog
- goose
- grouse
- gull
- hawk
- horse
- hound
- lion
- louse
- monkey
- parrot
- pig
- pigeon
- quail
- ram
- rat
- rook
- skunk
- snake
- snipe
- sponge
- squirrel
- toad
- weasel
- wolf
- worm

musculus

1. to brag about an accomplishment:
   to _____

2. stretch the neck for a better view:
   to _____

3. to imitate another's actions:
   to _____

4. to repeat another's words:
   to _____

5. to try to attract compliments:
   to _____

6. to lower the head quickly:
   to _____

7. to confuse somebody:
   to _____

8. to betray by spilling the beans:
   to _____

9. to intimidate: to _____

10. to annoy: to _____

11. to annoy: to _____

12. to cower: to _____

13. to strike violently: to _____

14. to eat a lot: to _____

15. to eat quickly: to _____

16. to struggle clumsily: to _____

17. to complain: to _____

18. to complain: to _____

19. to complain: to _____

20. to complain: to _____

21. to pursue relentlessly: to _____

22. to pursue relentlessly: to _____

23. to seek favor through flattery:

to _____

24. to cheat: to_____

25. to resist: to_____

26. to live off others: to _____

27. to dupe: to _____

28. to defeat soundly: to _____

29. to try to win over another's date:

to _____

30. to sell: to _____

31. to poke with the finger: to _____

32. to wind one's way: to _____

33. to outsmart: to out_____

34. to score two below par on a hole in golf:

to _____

35. to score one below par on a hole in golf:

to _____

36. to save: to _____ away

37. to flatter obsequiously: to _____y

38. to lose nerve: to _____ out

39. to become silent: to _____ up

40. to fool around: to _____around

41. to search for: to _____ out

42. to tamper with: to _____ with

43. to make a mistake: to _____ up

44. to force one's way: to _____
    through

45. to escape from a situation: to _____
    out of

46. to escape from a situation: to _____
    out of

47. to aim a snide attack: to _____ at

48. to categorize: to _____hole

49. to idolize: to _____ize

50. to jump over: to leap _____ over

(Answers on page 73)

◆ | Horsing Around

In modern life, horses no longer play a crucial role in helping us to hunt, do battle, draw vehicles, round up livestock, or deliver mail and goods. Nevertheless, our equine friends still figure prominently in the figures of speech that canter—neigh, gallop—through our language.

"Horsefeathers!" you respond, bridling at my suggestion and working yourself into a lather. "Now hold your horses and get off your high horse, you horse's ass. You're just trying to spur me on to the end of my tether and beat a dead horse." The meanings of these words and expressions are generally clear, although the equine expletive *horsefeathers* deserves an etymological exegesis. Rows of clapboards are laid on roofs to provide flat surfaces for asphalt shingles, called "feather strips." Old-timers in New England and New York, noting the featherlike pattern, called the clapboards horsefeathers. Why the *horse* in the word? Because the boards were large, and large things sometimes attract the designation *horse,* as in *horse chestnut, horse radish, horsefly,* and *horse mackerel.*

But why has *horsefeathers*—like *tommyrot, balderdash,* and *poppycock*—become a three-syllable explosion of derision? Because it has evolved into a euphemism for a shorter barnyard epithet. Check your dictionary and you'll discover a paddock of disguised words that descend from the world of horses, including *cavalier, cavalcade, chivalry, hackneyed, henchman, hippopotamus, marshal,* and any variation on the name *Philip.*

I'm full of horsepower and feeling my oats—champing (not chomping) at the bit and eager to give free rein to talking horse sense with you about the English language. So prick up your ears and listen to how often we compare people with horses—disk jockeys, coltish lasses with ponytails, dark-horse candidates who are groomed to give the front-runners and old war horses a run for their money, and workhorses who, although saddled with problems of galloping inflation, can't wait to get back in harness each Monday at the old stamping (not stomping) ground. Now, straight from the horse's mouth, here's a game in which you are asked to identify ten of the less obvious equine words and expressions stabled in our vocabulary. Learning the origins of these horsey phrases will help you to see that English is really a horse of a different color and not a mare's nest:

1. A horse is "rough-shoed" when the nails of its shoes project, ensuring a more surefooted progress but also damaging the ground over which it gallops. Thus, when we ruthlessly advance ourselves at other people's expense, we _____ over them.

2. Attendants groom and clean a horse's coat with a curry comb. When we wish someone to think well of us, we _____.

3. In an oft-used cliché we compare a point in time to a bespurred rider mounted upon our backs and urging us on with sharp prodding. This common expression is _____.

4. At the racetrack, notice boards display statistics for each horse. A fan who places bets that a given horse will win, place, or show has a better chance to gain cash by betting _____.

5. Jockeys urge their horses on by whispering "shoo" and shooing them on. Thus, a horse or a person who is an easy winner is known as a _____.

6. When a horse is so far ahead of the rest of the field that the outcome of the race is no longer in doubt, the jockey does not even have to lift the reins to urge his or her mount forward and wins _____.

7. Icy balls can become packed on the hooves of horses when they are driven over soft winter snow or during spring thaws. As the footing becomes treacherous, the horses may fall, singly or in teams, producing a state of affairs that is _____.

8. When is a holiday not a holiday? Back in the last century, when London omnibuses (whence our word *bus*) were horse-drawn, close relationships grew up between horse teams and their drivers. The regular driver would often spend his day off riding as a passenger alongside the substitute driver in order to check his replacement's handling of the horses. That's why a vacation or day off from work spent doing the same activity as one's usual work is called a _____.

9. When is a choice not a choice? Tobias Hobson (1544–1631), the owner of a Cambridge livery stable, gave his customers the dubious choice of taking a horse in its proper turn or taking none at all. To prevent the wearing down of his mounts, Hobson tolerated no picking and choosing, insisting that each rider take the first horse in line. Thus, when somebody offers you a _____, you are being offered no choice at all.

10. High-strung racehorses are sometimes given goats as stablemates to calm them, and the two animals can become inseparable companions. Certain gamblers have been known to steal the goat attached to a particular horse that they wanted to run poorly the next day. By _____, we today often affect someone's performance.

In this game, I've tried to lead a horse to language *and* make you think. I'm trusting that you won't look this gift horse in the mouth.

Don't look a gift horse in the mouth is one of the oldest

proverbs known to humankind, whinnying back at least 1,500 years. The age and health of a horse can be ascertained by examining the condition and number of its teeth. Although an animal may appear young and frisky, a close inspection may reveal that it is *long in the tooth* and ready for the glue factory. Still, it is considered bad manners to inspect the teeth of a horse that has been given you and, by extension, to inquire too closely into the cost or value of any gift.

If you are buying a horse from a trader, however, you are advised to determine whether it is a young stud or an old nag by examining the teeth *straight from the horse's mouth,* the precise source of this chapter.

(Answers on page 73)

♦ | ## DOG MY CATS!

The American love of cats and dogs pervades our language, and expressions involving these household pets abound in our speech and our writing. In this dog-eat-dog world of ours we meet top dogs who are doggone rich, underdogs in the doghouse, hot dogs who put on the dog, and dirty dogs who dog us with shaggy-dog stories, to say nothing of the pussyfooting cat's-paws, kittenish couples in puppy love, and cool cats sitting in the catbird seat. "Dog my cats!" we might say when it starts to rain cats and dogs. Then we may go inside and fight like you-know-whats.

Now that I've let the cat out of the bag, here are some statements about the felines and canines hiding in our language. In some cases the dog or cat in a word or phrase barks or meows clearly. The compound *dog days,* for example, which designates summer periods of hazy, hot, and humid weather, has a time-hallowed history. The Romans, who also experienced summer discomfiture, employed the expression *caniculares dies,* or "days of the dog," to describe the six to eight hottest weeks of the year. The ancient theory was that the dog star Sirius, rising with the sun during July and the first half of August, added to the solar heat and made a hot time even hotter. In other cases a dog or cat jumps out from a phrase and catches us by surprise. In a *caterpillar,* for example, hides "a hairy cat," from the Norman French word *catepelose.*

In still other cases a word or phrase bears no relationship to the words *cat* and *dog* beyond a mere coincidence of sound. But each word or word grouping in the game you are about to play does begin with the letters *c-a-t* or *d-o-g,* and these letters are pronounced exactly like the name of the animal, as in "This cat throws rocks at castles: *catapult.*"

1. This cat is a disaster. _____
2. This cat is a descriptive booklet.
   _____
3. This cat is a huge waterfall. _____
4. This cat tastes good on a hamburger.
   _____
5. This cat is classified. _____
6. This cat is cryptically buried underground.
   _____
7. This cat speeds a chemical reaction. ·
   _____
8. This cat chirps. _____
9. This cat swims. _____
10. This cat hopes one day to flutter by.
    _____
11. This cat is a narrow walkway.
    _____
12. This cat is a set of religious questions and
    answers. _____
13. This cat is a disaster. _____
14. This cat is a whip. _____
15. This cat is a short sleep. _____
16. This high-strung cat is in quite a few
    rackets. _____

17. This cat is a herd of beef. _____

18. This cat is a marsh plant. _____

19. This cat is a game with string.

_____

20. This cat walks on a diagonal line.

_____

21. This cat is a sailboat. _____

22. This cat is a harsh cry. _____

23. This cat is a gem. _____

24. This cat is a dupe, a tool of others.

_____

25. This cat is a type of mental illness.

_____

26. This cat is a type of mental illness.

_____

27. This cat is a place where one is "sitting
    pretty." _____

28. This cat is slang for "It's the greatest!"

_____

29. This cat is slang for "It's the greatest!"

_____

30. This cat is slang for "It's the greatest!"

_____

31. This cat is a three-dimensional X ray.

_____

32. This dog is an established set of beliefs.

_____

the cat's pajamas

33. This dog is another word for "darn."

———————————

34. This dog is a stretch of land that bends.

———————————

35. This dog swims underwater. ———————————

36. This dog is an elementary form of swimming. ———————————

37. L'il Abner lived in this dog. ———————————

38. This dog is clumsy verse. ———————————

39. This dog is shabby and worn. ———————————

40. This dog is exhausted. ———————————

41. This dog is a poisonous plant. ———————————

42. This dog is used for identification.

———————————

43. This dog is up a tree. ———————————

44. This dog is also up a tree. ———————————

45. This dog is a quick, easy gait. ———————————

46. This dog is a fiercely disputed contest.

———————————

(Answers on page 73)

◆ FOWL LANGUAGE

Not only is English a beastly language. It is for the birds.

To demonstrate that in our language words of a feather flock together, allow me just one exhibit—the crane. Even a birdbrain would have little trouble seeing how we derived the noun *crane* to describe a hoisting machine or the verb *to crane* to describe the act of stretching one's neck to obtain a better view. But it takes an eagle eye to spot the cranes hiding in *pedigree* and *cranberry*. *Pedigree* gets its pedigree from the French phrase *pied de grue,* "foot of a crane." Why? Because if you trace a pedigree on a genealogical table, you find that the lines of descent resemble a crane's foot. *Cranberries* take their name from the Low German *Kraanbere,* "crane berry," because cranes often inhabit the bogs where the berries flourish.

Take a gander at the aviary below to come up with appropriate words and expressions to match the definitions that follow. Sometimes the name of a given bird can stand by itself; sometimes you will have to provide a suffix or a phrase that includes a given bird, as in "low pay: *chickenfeed.*" Don't quail or duck this challenge. Feather your nest with all the correct answers you can, and you'll really have something to crow about:

◆
_____

THE AVIARY

_____
◆

- albatross
- buzzard
- canary
- catbird
- chicken
- cock
- coot
- crow
- cuckoo

- dodo
- dove
- duck
- eagle
- gander
- goose
- grouse
- gull
- hawk

- hen
- lark
- loon
- owl
- parrot
- pigeon
- turkey
- vulture

1. supporter of war
2. opponent of war
3. a coward
4. the wrong direction
5. a great burden
6. a parasitical person
7. a stupid person
8. a crazy person
9. a crazy person
10. an old person
11. an old person
12. dominated by one's wife
13. politician nearing end of term
14. one who stays up late
15. a position of advantage

16. aggressively confident
17. what humbled people eat
18. one who rats on others
19. one who rats on others
20. an escapade
21. look at
22. easily duped or cheated
23. having sharp sight
24. complain
25. suddenly, independently
26. repeat another's words

(Answers on page 74)

◆ EAT YOUR WORDS

In *The Philosophy of Rhetoric,* I. A. Richards notes: "The mind is a connecting organ. It works only by connecting and it can connect any two things in an indefinitely large number of ways." Making comparisons is a vital part of all language, and the metaphors that dominate the thoughts of a given culture are valuable clues to the way that culture perceives reality. One prominent value in our culture is the lively pursuit of the injunction to "eat, drink, and be merry." The next three games in this book are designed to reveal just how much the English language eats, drinks, and makes very merry.

The ancients knew that salt was essential to a good diet; for centuries before refrigeration it was the only chemical that could preserve meat. Thus, a portion of the wages paid to Roman soldiers was an allowance with which to buy salt (Latin, *sal*), and this stipend came to be called a *salarium,* from which English acquired the word *salary.* A loyal and effective soldier was quite literally *worth his salt.*

We think of carnivals as traveling entertainments with rides, side shows, games, cotton candy, and balloons, but the first carnivals were pre-Lenten celebrations—a last fling before penitence. The Latin word parts are *carne,* "meat, flesh," and *vale,* "farewell." The earliest carnivals were seasons of feasting and merrymaking, a "farewell to meat," just before Lent.

Companion and *company* derive from the sacred significance of breaking bread together, from the Latin *com,* "together," and *panis,* "bread." A companion, then, is a person with whom you share bread; when you have

eating your words

company at your home, you share your bread and hospitality. That wage earners are called breadwinners reminds us of the importance of bread in medieval life. Not surprisingly, both *lord* and *lady* are well-bread words. *Lord* descends from the Old English *hlaf*, "loaf," and *weard*, "keeper," and *lady* from *hlaf*, "loaf," and *dige*, "kneader."

So here's a toast to all those subtle culinary metaphors that add spice to our English language. Does that use of *toast* relate etymologically to the familiar slice of heated bread? In a word, yes. In Shakespeare's day it was common practice to place a piece of spiced or toasted bread in the bottom of one's wine or ale tankard to soak up impurities. The drink itself became "a toast," as did the gesture of drinking to another's good health.

Salt, meat, and bread are but three staples that season our English tongue, even if we are not always aware of their taste. Before you get fed up with this topic, select from the menu below to complete each savory expression that follows, as in "tempest in a *tea*pot":

♦
THE MENU

♦

• *apple*	• *cheese*	• *ham*
• *apple pie*	• *chestnut*	• *honey*
• *bacon*	• *clam*	• *hotcake*
• *banana*	• *cookie*	• *meat*
• *bean*	• *cucumber*	• *milk*
• *beer*	• *egg*	• *mincemeat*
• *beet*	• *fig*	• *molasses*
• *butter*	• *fish*	• *mustard*
• *cake*	• *fruitcake*	• *noodle*
• *candy*	• *grape*	• *nut*
• *cauliflower*	• *gravy*	• *oyster*

- *pancake*
- *pea*
- *peach*
- *peanut*
- *pickle*
- *pie*

- *potato*
- *pudding*
- *raspberry*
- *rhubarb*
- *salad*
- *salt*

- *sardine*
- *soup*
- *stuffing*
- *sugar*
- *tea*

1. not my cup of _____
2. the _____ of human kindness
3. _____ of the earth
4. the _____ train
5. go _____s
6. the _____ of his eye
7. _____ up the teacher
8. spill the _____s
9. crying in his _____
10. _____ order
11. a fine kettle of _____
12. in a _____
13. bring home the _____
14. giving him the _____
15. the proof of the _____
16. _____-coat the truth
17. _____y keen
18. _____ on her face
19. _____moon
20. cool as a _____
21. red as a _____
22. happy as a _____
23. flat as a _____

24. slow as _____

25. nutty as a _____

26. packed like _____s

27. selling like _____s

28. like taking _____ from a baby

29. like two _____s in a pod

30. can't cut the _____

31. duck _____

32. a couch _____

33. make _____ out of

34. beat the _____ out of

35. _____ it up

36. doesn't give a _____

37. a tough _____ to crack

38. working for _____s

39. _____cloth

40. through the _____vine

41. an argument in baseball: _____

42. It's a piece of _____.

43. Use your _____.

44. a smart _____

45. He's dead _____.

46. _____ in the sky

47. an old _____

48. _____ ear

49. in one's _____ days

50. The world is her _____.

(Answers on page 74)

◆ # FACE THE MUSIC

About three thousand years ago, clowns would smack one another with paddles made of two wooden laths. When they were slapped together, these paddles produced a loud whacking sound and a delighted audience. Eventually the instrument came to be known as a slapstick, and soon the name was applied to any knockabout farce.

The English poet and playwright John Dennis is most remembered for two comments. It was he who first sneered, "A pun is the lowest form of wit." And for his tragedy *Appius and Virginia* (a tragic failure with the critics in 1709) Dennis invented a device to generate the roaring of thunder as part of the staging. Shortly after the play's premature closing, he heard his own thunder machine roar during the witches' scene in a production of *Macbeth*. "My God!" the upstaged Dennis exclaimed. "The villains will steal my thunder but not play my plays!" And that's where we get the expression *steal my thunder*.

After people eat and drink they often make merry. Because entertainment is so joyful and enriching, show business metaphors help our language to get its act together and get the show on the road. At the right time, these lively figures stop waiting in the wings and step out into the limelight. The first limelights were theatrical spotlights that used heated calcium oxide, or quicklime, to give off a brilliant white light. Ever since that bright idea, *to be in the limelight* has been a metaphor for being in the glare of public scrutiny.

Most actors experience a touch of stage fright at the moment of going onstage. But, looking out across the

orchestra pit, each actor must eventually go into the limelight and *face the music,* as I now ask you to do.

William Shakespeare began his comedy *Twelfth Night*
with the line "If music be the food of love, play on."
About a century later, William Congreve penned the
equally famous line: "Music hath charms to soothe a
savage breast" (often misquoted as "the savage beast").
You don't have to be a great writer to notice how nourish-
ing and charming music is in our lives. But have you ever
thought about how many musical words and phrases
resonate in our language?

When we talk about someone trying *to soft-pedal*
something, we are referring to the pedal on a piano that is
used to mute tone. Thus, when we soft-pedal an idea, we
make it less emphatic or obvious and we moderate and
play it down. If, on the other hand, we do the opposite
and *pull out all the stops,* we are acting like the organist
who pulls out all the stops, or knobs, in the instrument to
bring all the pipes into play.

Before you complain that I'm fiddling around and
horning in on you, try tuning in to a low-key quiz. You'll
find that the English language will be fit as a fiddle and
music to your ears.

Complete the common phrases with the musical
terms in the box:

_____ ♦ _____

MELODIOUS WORDS

_____ ♦ _____

• *band*	• *dance*	• *horn*
• *bandwagon*	• *drum*	• *jazz*
• *beat*	• *fiddle*	• *key*
• *chime*	• *fiddlesticks*	• *note*
• *chord*	• *harmony*	• *opera*
• *chorus*	• *harp*	• *orchestrate*

- *overture*
- *pipe*
- *piper*
- *piping*
- *pitch*

- *play*
- *polka*
- *ring*
- *song*
- *sung*

- *trumpet*
- *tune*
- *whistling*

1. hop on the _____
2. play second _____
3. a soap _____
4. blow your own _____
5. make an _____ to the opposition
6. Don't give me a _____ and _____
7. Don't _____ on the subject.
8. laughing to beat the _____
9. strike a responsive _____
10. _____ in during a discussion
11. reach a fever _____
12. in _____ with the times
13. _____ up business
14. a _____ of boos
15. You're just _____ Dixie.
16. an up_____ attitude
17. pay the _____
18. _____ ! I don't believe it!
19. a key_____ speaker
20. a _____ing elephant

a soap opera

21. exist in perfect _____

22. all that _____

23. _____ it by ear

24. _____ hot

25. _____ dots

26. _____ in the new year

27. an un_____ hero

28. _____ a complicated plan

29. all _____ed up

30. Please _____ down!

(Answers on page 75)

♦ | THE SPORTY ENGLISH LANGUAGE

Walt Whitman wrote that "language is not an abstract construction of the learned, or of dictionary makers, but is something arising out of the work, needs, ties, joys, affections, tastes of long generations of humanity." Because sports occupy such a central place in American life and imagination, athletic metaphors pervade our everyday speech and writing. There is indeed a kind of democratic poetry in the sporty metaphors that make our English language so athletic, and these metaphors are vivid emblems of the games that we, as a people, watch and play.

Take the language of politics. An observer of American political life cannot help but be struck by the profusion of horse racing and track metaphors that shape our thinking about campaigns and elections. Some candidates are dark horses champing at the bit to make a stretch run; others are frontrunners whose track records give them the inside track on the nomination; still others are shoo-ins who take the whole thing in stride. In some campaigns the pacesetters stumble trying to clear the initial hurdles, and those back in the pack give them a good run for the money. Then the contest turns into a real horse race—a marathon that may go right down to the wire.

When candidates enter a political race, they "throw their hat in the ring." This popular expression, dating back to the nineteenth century, is said to spring from the custom of throwing a hat in a boxing ring to signal acceptance of a pugilist's challenge. Straight from the shoulder, boxing metaphors pull no punches in our language. When fate has us on the ropes and is hitting us with low blows in a knockdown, dragout fight, we can take it on the chin, get knocked for a loop, go down for the count, or throw in the towel or sponge; or we can roll with the punches, beat our opponent to the punch, come out swinging, or be saved by the bell.

In the early days of the twentieth century a college professor explained, "To understand America, you must first understand baseball." Baseball is not only America's pastime but the most pervasive athletic metaphor in the American language. Right off the bat we bat around a few ideas and then go to bat for someone. If we don't touch base with others, we may find ourselves way off base or not able to get to first base.

Please don't think me a screwball who's out in left field with two strikes against me. I'm playing linguistic hardball here, and I call 'em as I see 'em. And what I see are ballpark figures like *in there pitching, bush league operation, major league performance, play the field, a smash hit, safe by a mile, to take a rain check, hit and run,* and *to pinch-hit* for somebody.

Even more exotic sports, such as cockfighting, contribute to the poetry of our prose. From the cockpit (yes, the modern meaning of the word comes from the cramped arena of flying feathers) we gain several common metaphors. A hackle is a long, narrow, shiny feather on the necks of certain birds, gamecocks among them. In the heat of battle, a fighting cock's hackles become erect as a demonstration of its fury. That's why, when the going gets rough, people *get their hackles up.* If that going gets too rough, people can become crestfallen. *Crestfallen,* meaning "dispirited or defeated," does not refer to the act of dropping one's toothpaste. As victory approaches, the crest of a fighting cock rises, deep red and rigid. But when defeat is imminent, the crest droops—and the bird becomes crestfallen.

Okay, sport, the ball is now in your court. How many sports and games can you find hidden in the following game plan?

> *When the chips are down, the situation is up for grabs, and some well-heeled opponent is tossing us a red herring, we must knuckle down, hold the line, call the shots, hit the bull's-eye, get on a roll, get the ball rolling, take the bull by the horns with no holds barred, and put the ball in the other guy's court. Otherwise, we may end up jumping the gun, not up to par, down and out, out in left field, behind the eight ball, barking up the wrong tree, coming a cropper, taking the bait hook, line, and sinker, and facing a sticky wicket.*

(Answers on page 75)

♦ # Answers

Body Language
(page 3)

1. eye **2.** bone **3.** heart **4.** head **5.** mouth **6.** leg
7. tongue **8.** body **9.** neck **10.** thumb

11. spleen **12.** rib **13.** ear **14.** chest **15.** shoulder
16. chin **17.** gut **18.** knee **19.** elbow **20.** lip

21. foot **22.** toe **23.** knuckle **24.** skeleton **25.** breast
26. throat **27.** artery **28.** nose **29.** back **30.** tooth/nail

31. lung **32.** hair **33.** intestin(e) **34.** brow **35.** hand
36. craw **37.** limb/limb **38.** cheek **39.** stomach **40.** flesh

41. whisker **42.** brain **43.** face **44.** heel **45.** arm
46. finger **47.** liver **48.** spine or gut **49.** belly **50.** scalp

Heartfelt Words
(page 10)

1. take to heart **2.** have a heart **3.** sweetheart **4.** take
heart **5.** have one's heart set on **6.** have one's heart in one's
mouth **7.** disheartened **8.** halfhearted **9.** wholehearted
10. hearty

11. heartache **12.** heart of the matter, at the heart of
13. lionhearted **14.** heart isn't in it **15.** have one's heart in the
right place **16.** cross one's heart **17.** heart of gold, good-
hearted **18.** heartless, heart of stone, hardhearted
19. heartthrob **20.** lose heart

21. eat one's heart out **22.** bleeding heart **23.** learn by heart **24.** heartburn **25.** play one's heart out **26.** after my own heart **27.** change of heart **28.** put one's heart at rest **29.** the heartbeat **30.** young at heart

31. to have one's heart in one's throat **32.** heart-to-heart **33.** blackhearted **34.** lighthearted **35.** heart-stopping

CLOTHES MAKE THE LANGUAGE

(page 13)

1. sleeve **2.** collar **3.** button **4.** britches or breeches **5.** coat **6.** boot **7.** hood **8.** shirt **9.** apron **10.** jacket

11. gown **12.** clothing **13.** vest **14.** wig **15.** bonnet **16.** cloak **17.** cap **18.** pocket **19.** hairpin **20.** veil

21. necktie **22.** glove **23.** cuff **24.** pajamas **25.** shoe **26.** pants **27.** jock or socks **28.** stocking **29.** shoestring **30.** belt

31. coattails **32.** bootstraps **33.** hat **34.** buttonhole **35.** nightcap

HOUSEHOLD WORDS

(page 17)

1. stool **2.** soap **3.** rocker **4.** blanket **5.** saucer **6.** curtain **7.** basket **8.** pot **9.** razor **10.** sieve

11. bed **12.** kettle **13.** pan **14.** barrel **15.** carpet **16.** armchair **17.** spoon **18.** cradle **19.** snuff **20.** chair

21. bucket **22.** comb **23.** kitchen sink **24.** book **25.** candle **26.** table **27.** iron **28.** hammer **29.** tack **30.** wringer

31. can **32.** rug **33.** light **34.** button **35.** picture **36.** sandpaper **37.** board **38.** sheet **39.** nail **40.** putty

41. drawer **42.** dish **43.** screwdriver **44.** mousetrap **45.** clock **46.** key **47.** purse **48.** saw **49.** monkey wrench **50.** doormat

COLORFUL ENGLISH

(page 22)

1. black **2.** blue **3.** green **4.** yellow **5.** blue **6.** gold
7. blue **8.** gray **9.** blue **10.** red

11. blue **12.** red **13.** purple **14.** silver **15.** brown
16. red **17.** rose **18.** lime **19.** black/blue **20.** pink

21. green **22.** gold **23.** black **24.** red **25.** blue
26. green **27.** red **28.** black **29.** red **30.** blue

31. gold **32.** white **33.** brown **34.** blue **35.** brown
36. yellow **37.** black **38.** red **39.** gray **40.** blue

41. red **42.** green **43.** Black **44.** White **45.** red
46. blue **47.** blue **48.** gray **49.** brown **50.** pink

Among the words that describe both a color and an object are:
gold, green, lemon, lilac, lime, olive, peach, plum, rose, salmon,
silver, slate, tangerine, and violet.

DOWN-TO-EARTH METAPHORS

(page 27)

1. furrowed **2.** cultivated **3.** harrowing **4.** delirium, delirious **5.** aftermath **6.** windfall **7.** a hard (or tough) row to hoe **8.** nip it in the bud **9.** make hay while the sun shines **10.** goes haywire

SEAWORTHY METAPHORS

(page 31)

1. nausea **2.** nave **3.** leeway **4.** scuttlebutt **5.** touch and go **6.** hard and fast **7.** in the doldrums **8.** left high and dry **9.** taking them down a peg **10.** the devil and the deep blue sea **11.** three sheets in (to) the wind **12.** the bitter end

WEATHER OR NOT

(page 35)

1. gale **2.** tempest **3.** thunder **4.** lightning **5.** sunny **6.** bolt **7.** slush **8.** snow **9.** whirlwind **10.** flood

11. frozen   12. breeze   13. storm   14. ice   15. wind
16. rain   17. hazy or foggy   18. fog   19. cloud   20. heat
21. shower   22. cool   23. misty   24. climate

BEASTLY ENGLISH

(page 39)

1. crow   2. crane   3. ape   4. parrot   5. fish   6. duck
7. buffalo   8. rat   9. cow   10. badger
11. bug   12. quail   13. ram   14. pig   15. wolf
16. flounder   17. bitch   18. carp   19. crab   20. grouse
21. dog   22. hound   23. fawn   24. rook   25. buck
26. sponge   27. gull   28. skunk   29. bird dog   30. hawk
31. goose   32. snake   33. fox   34. eagle   35. bird
36. squirrel   37. toad   38. chicken   39. clam   40. horse
41. ferret   42. monkey   43. louse   44. bull   45. weasel
46. worm   47. snipe   48. pigeon   49. lion   50. frog

HORSING AROUND

(page 45)

1. ride roughshod   2. curry favor   3. spur of the moment
4. across the board   5. shoo-in   6. hands down   7. all balled
up   8. busman's holiday   9. Hobson's choice   10. getting his
goat

DOG MY CATS!

(page 49)

1. catastrophe   2. catalog   3. cataract   4. catsup
5. category   6. catacomb   7. catalyst   8. catbird   9. catfish
10. caterpillar
11. catwalk   12. catechism   13. cataclysm
14. cat-o'-nine-tails   15. catnap   16. catgut   17. cattle
18. cattail   19. cat's cradle   20. catercorner
21. catamaran   22. caterwaul   23. cat's-eye   24. cat's-paw
25. catalepsy   26. catatonia   27. catbird seat   28. cat's meow
29. cat's pajamas   30. cat's whiskers   31. CAT scan

32. dogma   33. doggone   34. dogleg   35. dogfish
36. dog paddle   37. Dogpatch   38. doggerel   39. dog-eared
40. dog tired
    41. dogbane   42. dog tag   43. dogberry   44. dogwood
45. dogtrot   46. dogfight

FOWL LANGUAGE

(page 54)

1. hawk   2. dove   3. chicken   4. wild goose chase
5. albatross   6. vulture   7. dodo   8. cuckoo   9. loon
10. buzzard
    11. coot   12. henpecked   13. lame duck   14. night owl
15. in the catbird seat   16. cocky or cocksure   17. crow
18. canary   19. stool pigeon   20. lark
    21. take a gander at   22. gullible   23. eagle-eyed
24. grouse   25. cold turkey   26. parrot

EAT YOUR WORDS

(page 57)

1. tea   2. milk   3. salt   4. gravy   5. banana   6. apple
7. butter   8. bean   9. beer   10. apple pie
    11. fish   12. pickle (or jam or stew)   13. bacon
14. raspberry   15. pudding   16. sugar   17. peach   18. egg
19. honey   20. cucumber
    21. beet (or lobster)   22. clam   23. pancake   24. molasses
25. fruitcake   26. sardine   27. hotcake   28. candy   29. pea
30. mustard
    31. soup   32. potato   33. mincemeat   34. stuffing
35. ham   36. fig   37. nut   38. peanut   39. cheese   40. grape
    41. rhubarb   42. cake   43. noodle   44. cookie   45. meat
46. pie   47. chestnut   48. cauliflower   49. salad   50. oyster

FACE THE MUSIC

(page 62)

1. bandwagon **2.** fiddle **3.** opera **4.** horn **5.** overture
6. song/dance **7.** harp **8.** band **9.** chord **10.** chime or horn
11. pitch **12.** tune **13.** drum **14.** chorus **15.** whistling
16. beat **17.** piper **18.** Fiddlesticks **19.** note **20.** trumpet
21. harmony **22.** jazz **23.** play **24.** piping **25.** polka
26. ring **27.** sung **28.** orchestrate **29.** key **30.** pipe

THE SPORTY ENGLISH LANGUAGE

(page 67)

Twenty-two sports and games are represented:

When the chips are down *(poker)*, the situation is up for grabs *(basketball)*, and some well-heeled *(cockfighting)* opponent is tossing us a red herring *(fox hunting)*, we must knuckle down *(marbles)*, hold the line *(football)*, call the shots *(billiards)*, hit the bulls-eye *(archery)*, get on a roll *(dicing)*, get the ball rolling *(soccer)*, take the bull by the horns *(rodeo)* with no holds barred *(wrestling)*, and put the ball in the other guy's court *(tennis)*. Otherwise, we may end up jumping the gun *(track)*, not up to par *(golf)*, down and out *(boxing)*, out in left field *(baseball)*, behind the eight ball *(pool)*, barking up the wrong tree *(coon hunting)*, coming a cropper *(horse racing)*, taking the bait hook, line, and sinker (fishing), and facing a sticky wicket *(cricket)*.

II

CLICHÉS

"Adam was the only man who, when he said a good thing, knew that nobody had said it before him."

—MARK TWAIN

◆ CUT AND DRIED CLICHÉS

A girl was asked by her teacher to use the word *cliché* in a sentence. She responded with this statement: "The boy returned home from the test with a cliché on his face." When the teacher asked her to explain herself, the girl pointed out that the dictionary defines *cliché* as "a worn-out expression."

A cliché is indeed a worn-out expression, so threadbare that it has become completely predictable. Offer the first half of such a phrase, and instantly in the minds of almost everybody flashes the second half. If, for example, I say, "beck," most English speakers will respond with the knee-jerk "and call." If I say, "cut," as in the title of this chapter, the fill-in will inevitably be "and dried." *Cut and dried* is actually a very dead metaphor. Certain herbs sold in herbalists' shops were displayed in a preserved form rather than being newly picked. Since the early seventeenth century these products have been labeled "cut and dried"; by extension we today use the label to refer to anything lacking freshness and spontaneity.

The very fact that the second halves of such expressions skip so easily into the mind is a danger signal. It means that everyone else would use the same turn of phrase, a perfect recipe for triteness.

Identifying clichés is an exercise guaranteed to keep you up to par, up to scratch, and up to snuff, rather than up in arms, up a tree, and up the creek; in clover, in the groove, in the pink, and in like Flynn, rather than in the doghouse, in hot water, in a pickle, and in a rut; and on the ball, on the beam, on the go, on the level, on the make, on the up-and-up, and on the wagon, rather than on the bottle, on the fly, on the carpet, on the fence, on the fritz, on the rocks, on the ropes, and on the spot.

Here's a warm-up game that will help you to keep your eyes peeled, your fingers crossed, your nose to the grindstone, your shoulder to the wheel, your ear to the ground, and your head above water. Supply the missing parts of each very worn-out expression:

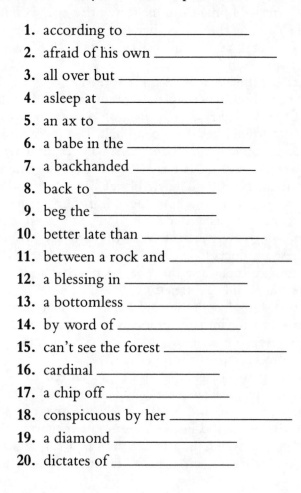

   1. according to _____

   2. afraid of his own _____

   3. all over but _____

   4. asleep at _____

   5. an ax to _____

   6. a babe in the _____

   7. a backhanded _____

   8. back to _____

   9. beg the _____

 10. better late than _____

 11. between a rock and _____

 12. a blessing in _____

 13. a bottomless _____

 14. by word of _____

 15. can't see the forest _____

 16. cardinal _____

 17. a chip off _____

 18. conspicuous by her _____

 19. a diamond _____

 20. dictates of _____

21. fits and _____
22. for all intents and _____
23. a foregone _____
24. grin and _____
25. hand over _____
26. here today, _____
27. hue and _____
28. in the twinkling of _____
29. a last-ditch _____
30. a new lease _____
31. a load off _____
32. make both ends _____
33. might and _____
34. the naked _____
35. odds and _____
36. pure and _____
37. sadder but _____
38. so far, _____
39. spitting _____
40. a square peg _____
41. stark raving _____
42. start from _____
43. take it or _____
44. too good to be _____
45. throw down the _____
46. when all is said and _____
47. the whole ball of _____

48. wishful _____

49. worn to a _____

50. wreak _____

(Answers on page 121)

♦ TRITE AS A CLICHÉ

The earliest clichés were printing plates, or stereotypes, made first from wood, then clay, and, finally, cast from metal. The figurative sense of clichés and stereotypes arose later because these plates were often reused and were impervious to change.

One of the ironies of language is that striking figures of speech and vivid comparisons soon become clichés precisely because they initially express an idea so well. These phrases catch on, are picked up by a host of people, and quickly become trite or dead as their originality and cleverness vanish into thin air (itself a cliché).

The English novelist and critic George Orwell used another figure of speech to express the prevailing triteness of modern writing. He contended that "prose consists less and less of words chosen for the sake of their meaning, and more and more of phrases tacked together like the sections of a prefabricated henhouse."

Take the hackneyed formula "(adjective) as a (noun)." Out of hurry or habit many speakers and writers press into service these stale, formulaic phrases without much regard for their meanings. We call somebody *happy as a clam*, for example, without having any idea of what's so happy about clams.

Digging into this particular cliché, the whimsical poet Ogden Nash once composed this little ditty:

> *The clam, esteemed by gourmets highly*
> *Is said to live the life of Riley.*
> *When you are lolling on a piazza,*
> *It's what you are as happy as a.*

But the question lingers: Why should this helpless bivalve—captive in its shell until pried open and steamed, baked, minced, stuffed, or casinoed by humans—be happy?

As it turns out, *happy as a clam* is only half the original saying. The full simile is "happy as a clam at high tide." A clam at high tide is quite sensibly happy because, at that time, the mud flat in which it buries itself is safe from human invasion.

When we describe someone as *smart as a whip,* we are likely to make him or her feel *pleased as punch.* But what is so smart about a whip, and why should punch be pleased?

Delving into the history of *smart,* we find that the word first meant "experiencing sharp pain." Gradually the adjective took on additional meanings, including "quick, active, and prompt," as in "look smart!" and, by extension, "clever, intelligent." *Smart as a whip* unites the older and newer meanings.

The punch that is so pleased in the cliché is not the stuff we drink, but the Punch of the Punch and Judy shows, created in the early seventeenth century. While most people believe that *pleased as Punch* is a food metaphor (and hence neglect to capitalize the *P*), the phrase in fact alludes to the cheerful singing and self-satisfaction of the extroverted puppet.

May you be pleased as the Punch of Punch and Judy and happy as a clam at high tide when you review the "(adjective) as a (noun)" clichés that follow. Complete the first set of trite comparisons by inserting the names of animals:

1. bald as _____
2. blind as _____
3. brave as _____
4. busy as _____

blind as a bat

5. busy as _____

6. clean as _____

7. crazy as _____

8. crazy as _____

9. crazy as _____

10. cross as _____

11. cute as _____

12. drunk as _____

13. dumb as _____

14. fat as _____

15. free as _____

16. gentle as _____

17. hairy as _____

18. happy as _____

19. happy as _____

20. healthy as _____

21. hungry as _____

22. loose as _____

23. mad as _____

24. mad as _____

25. naked as _____

26. nervous as _____

27. plump as _____

28. poor as _____

29. proud as _____

30. quiet as _____

31. red as _____

32. scarce as _____

33. sick as _____

34. silly as _____

35. slippery as _____

36. sly as _____

37. snug as _____

38. strong as _____

39. strong as _____

40. stubborn as _____

41. tight as _____

42. wise as _____

Complete the following by using other things found in nature:

43. big as _____

44. clear as _____

45. cold as _____

46. easy as _____

47. fast as _____

48. fresh as _____

49. good as _____

50. green as _____

51. hard as _____

52. hot as _____

53. light as _____

54. old as _____

55. pure as _____

fast as lightning

56. right as _____

57. solid as _____

58. sturdy as _____

Complete the following by using types of food:

59. American as _____

60. brown as _____

61. cool as _____

62. easy as _____

63. flat as _____

64. nutty as _____

65. red as _____

66. slow as _____

67. soft as _____

68. sweet as _____

69. sweet as _____

70. thick as _____

71. warm as _____

72. wrinkled as _____

Complete the following by using objects found around the house:

73. bald as _____

74. big as _____

75. black as _____

76. black as _____

77. comfortable as _____

78. cute as _____

79. dead as _____

80. deaf as _____

81. dry as _____

82. dull as _____

83. funny as _____

84. high as _____

85. hot as _____

86. limp as _____

87. neat as _____

88. pale as _____

89. pretty as _____

90. rough as _____

91. sharp as _____

92. smooth as _____

93. stiff as _____

94. soft as _____

95. thin as _____

96. tight as _____

97. tight as _____

98. tough as _____

99. tough as _____

100. white as _____

Now, for a change in approach, fill in the first part of each cliché by inserting the appropriately hackneyed adjective:

101. ——————————— as an arrow
102. ——————————— as a bell
103. ——————————— as a bone
104. ——————————— as Croesus
105. ——————————— as day
106. ——————————— as the day is long
107. ——————————— as the day you were born
108. ——————————— as Dick's hatband
109. ——————————— as a dollar
110. ——————————— as a fiddle
111. ——————————— as a flash
112. ——————————— as a hatter
113. ——————————— as a judge
114. ——————————— as life
115. ——————————— as a lord
116. ——————————— as Methusaleh
117. ——————————— as a newborn babe
118. ——————————— as night and day
119. ——————————— as the nose on your face
120. ——————————— as a pistol
121. ——————————— as a rail
122. ——————————— as shootin'
123. ——————————— as sin
124. ——————————— as thieves

125. _____ as a three-dollar bill
126. _____ as a tomb
127. _____ as a whistle
128. _____ as a wink

(Answers on page 121)

◆ AVOID CLICHÉS LIKE THE PLAGUE

Now that you know your *as* from a hole in the ground, let's move on to a more *like*ly story. Some of these clichés make more literal sense than others. We might say of two people that they *fight like cats and dogs,* a sensible simile given the noisy battles of cats and dogs. On the other hand, we might accuse somebody of *drinking like a fish* without realizing that fish really don't drink all that much, even if they appear to.

Like is a preposition you can't refuse in our language. In many of the sixty-five clichés that follow, it is also a conjunction—and that's *telling it like it is.* Complete each *like*ly expression, and you'll be *in like Flynn* (who was a real 1940s New York politician), not *out like a light:*

1. blew up like _____

2. built like _____

3. built like _____

4. came out smelling like _____

5. cleans like _____

6. clever like _____

7. come on like _____

8. cried like _____

9. dropped it like _____

10. dropping like _____

11. eats like _____

12. eats like _____

13. eats like _____

14. Finding the lost coin is like _____.

15. fits like _____

16. fix it like _____

17. Getting an answer out of her is like

_____.

18. Getting an answer out of him is like

_____.

19. I know this place like _____.

20. grew like _____

21. grew like _____

22. He needs it like _____.

23. hit him like _____

24. lie like _____

25. lit up like _____

26. live like _____

27. make out like _____

28. March comes in like _____ 29. and out like _____ .

30. melts like _____

31. a memory like _____

32. a memory like _____

33. a mind like _____

34. The news spread like _____.

35. rolls off him like _____

36. runs around like _____

37. runs like _____

38. runs like _____

39. sank like _____

40. selling like ————————

41. shaking like ————————

42. She looks great; she looks like ————————.

43. She looks awful; she looks like ————————.

44. She took to it like ————————.

45. She took to it like ————————.

46. slept like ————————

47. slept like ————————

48. slept like ————————

49. smokes like ————————

smokes like a chimney

50. soars like _____

51. spends money like _____

52. sticks out like _____

53. stole away like _____

54. swears like _____

55. They passed like _____.

56. They're so alike they're like _____.

57. took to it like _____

58. treat like _____

59. wails like _____

60. watch like _____

61. went off like _____

62. went on and on like _____

63. went over like _____

64. works like _____

65. works like _____

(Answers on page 122)

♦ DYNAMIC TRIOS

The number three has held great power and fascination for humankind through the centuries. We think about time as past, present, and future; we divide our days into morning, afternoon, and night and our meals into breakfast, lunch, and dinner.

For the ancient Greeks, Zeus ruled the sky with his three-forked lightning bolt, Poseidon the sea with his trident, and Hades the underworld, which was guarded by Cerberus, the three-headed dog. Greek mythology is populated by three fates, three furies, three graces, and three harpies. The Greek philosopher Aristotle theorized that all works of literature should have a beginning, middle, and end and should adhere to the three unities of time, place, and plot.

In the Old Testament we read about the patriarchs Abraham, Isaac, and Jacob, the three days that Jonah lived in the whale, and the three lions that Daniel met. In the New Testament we learn of the Trinity, the three wise men, the three victims crucified, the three denials of Peter, and the resurrection of Jesus three days after his death at the oft-cited age of thirty-three. In Hinduism there are Brahma, the creator; Vishnu, the preserver; and Siva, the destroyer.

In popular literature we meet all sorts of threesomes ranging from the three witches in *Macbeth* and three daughters in *King Lear* to the three musketeers, the three bears, the three little pigs, and the three blind mice.

Now consider another hundred famous triplets— threesomes that often hang around together, like our three primary colors—red, blue, and yellow. In each of the dynamic trios, I have supplied the last item. Complete each triad by supplying the first two.

We'll start with triple plays arranged in the most common patter—*a, b,* and *c:*

1. _____, _____, and able
2. _____, _____, and apple pie
3. _____, _____, and away
4. _____, _____, and baby bear
5. _____, _____, and barrel
6. _____, _____, and be merry
7. _____, _____, and beads
8. _____, _____, and blue
9. _____, _____, and candle
10. _____, _____, and charity
11. _____, _____, and Chevrolet
12. _____, _____, and child
13. _____, _____, and clothing
14. _____, _____, and collected
15. _____, _____, and Corinthian
16. _____, _____, and delivered
17. _____, _____, and evermore shall be
18. _____, _____, and everywhere
19. _____, _____, and first in the hearts of his countrymen
20. _____, _____, and for the people
21. _____, _____, and gas
22. _____, _____, and handsome

23. _____, _____, and handsome

24. _____, _____, and happy

25. _____, _____, and Holy Ghost

26. _____, _____, and I

27. _____, _____, and in the air

28. _____, _____, and in my lady's chamber

29. _____, _____, and judicial

30. _____, _____, and a jump

31. _____, _____, and listen

32. _____, _____, and myrrh

33. _____, _____, and neuter

34. _____, _____, and nothing but the truth

35. _____, _____, and obey

36. _____, _____, and pop

37. _____, _____, and potentates

38. _____, _____, and the pursuit of happiness

39. _____, _____, and 'rithmetic

40. _____, _____, and rock 'n' roll

41. _____, _____, and roll

42. _____, _____, and scalene

43. _____, _____, and serial number

44. _____, _____, and sinker

45. _____, _____, and song

46. _____, _____, and spoon

47. _____, _____, and stars

48. _____, _____, and superego
49. _____, _____, and tattooed
50. _____, _____, and tears
51. _____, _____, and throat
52. _____, _____, and tomato
53. _____, _____, *and the Ugly*
54. _____, _____, *and the Wardrobe*
55. _____, _____, and yon

Just between you, me, and the gate post (grammatically incorrect but still another triple play), many more dynamic trios occur in slightly different patterns—*a, b, c; a* and *b* and *c;* and *a, b,* or *c.* Again you are to supply the first two items:

56. _____! _____! action!
57. _____ and _____ and bears
58. no _____, _____, or buts
59. _____, _____ , the candlestick maker
60. _____ _____ c's
61. _____, _____, countrymen
62. _____, _____, or draw
63. _____ and _____ and everything nice
64. _____! _____! fire!
65. _____, _____, or form
66. _____, _____, fraternity
67. _____! _____! go!
68. _____! _____! go!
69. _____! _____! gone!

70. _____, _____, Indian chief
71. _____, _____, or indifferent
72. _____! _____! It's Superman!
73. _____, _____, or milk
74. _____, _____, or mineral
75. _____, _____, or mutilate
76. _____ and _____, and puppy dog tails
77. _____, _____, scissors
78. _____, _____, or show
79. _____, _____, or snow
80. _____, _____, speak no evil
81. _____, _____, or steal
82. _____, _____, thank you ma'am
83. _____, _____, or thing
84. _____ _____ toe
85. _____, _____, vici

Becoming more proper in our choice of nouns, let's move on to some famous names that help make the trinitty-gritty of our language. In each case, supply the first two names:

86. _____, _____, and Abednego
87. _____, _____, and Aramis
88. _____, _____, and Balthasar
89. _____ to _____, to Chance
90. _____, _____, and Cottontail
91. _____, _____, and Harry
92. _____, _____, and Jack

Kukla, Fran, and Ollie

93. _____, _____, and Jutes
94. _____, _____, and Louie
95. _____, _____, and Mary
96. _____, _____, and Nash
97. _____, _____, and Nod
98. _____, _____, and Ollie
99. _____, _____, and the Santa Fe
100. _____, _____, and the *Santa Maria*

(Answers on page 123)

♦ ## WHOSE WHAT?

English is a highly possessive language: We have so many expressions concocted from the formula *whose what* that we could run the gamut from *A* to *Z* several times. Beginning at *A,* we have *Adam's apple,* so called because many men, but few women, exhibit a bulge of laryngeal cartilage in front of their throats. According to male-dominated folklore, Eve swallowed her apple without care or residue while a chunk of the fruit stuck in the throat of the misled and basically honest Adam. Ending with *Z,* we have *Zeno's paradoxes,* a series of eight brainbusters posed by the Greek philosopher Zeno of Elea (*c.* 495–430 B.C.). The most famous of Zeno's posers to survive goes like this: Achilles sees a tortoise moving slowly ahead in the distance and sets out to catch up with it. But when he reaches point A, where he first saw the tortoise, the animal has moved ahead to point B. And when Achilles gets to B, the tortoise has progressed to point C. Therefore, no matter how determinedly or swiftly Achilles races ahead, he can never catch up with the tortoise.

I'm confident that you can catch up with more than a hundred and fifty *Whose what's.* The first section of the game involves animals. Supply the noun that follows each zoological possessive, as in rabbit's *foot:*

1. a bird's _____
2. bull's _____
3. cat's _____
4. cat's _____

5. the cat's _____
6. the cat's _____
7. the cat's _____
8. in a coon's _____
9. crow's _____
10. crow's _____
11. a dog's _____
12. frog's _____
13. scarce as hens' _____
14. a hornet's _____
15. a horse's _____
16. the lion's _____
17. a mare's _____
18. a monkey's _____
19. in a pig's _____
20. at a snail's _____

For the next grouping, again supply a noun that follows each possessive:

21. at arm's _____
22. athlete's _____
23. baby's _____
24. baker's _____
25. beginner's _____
26. blind man's _____
27. the bum's _____
28. businessman's _____
29. busman's _____

30. cheater's _____
31. chef's _____
32. chef's _____
33. child's _____
34. citizen's _____
35. collector's _____
36. all in a day's _____
37. dead man's _____
38. dean's _____
39. at death's _____
40. debtor's _____
41. devil's _____
42. doctor's _____
43. your father's _____
44. finder's _____
45. fireman's _____
46. fool's _____
47. fool's _____
48. fool's _____
49. gentleman's _____
50. gentlemen's _____
51. God's _____
52. a hair's _____
53. in harm's _____
54. heart's _____
55. heart's _____
56. for heaven's _____
57. Hell's _____

58. Hell's_____

59. housemaid's _____

60. idiot's _____

61. Jehovah's _____

62. a king's _____

63. the King's _____

64. ladies' _____

65. ladies' _____

66. the Lord's _____

67. lovers' _____

68. lovers' _____

69. lovers' _____

70. mama's _____

71. the mind's _____

72. mother's _____

73. mother's _____

74. murderers' _____

75. no-man's _____

76. old wives' _____

77. painter's _____

78. potter's _____

79. potter's _____

80. printer's _____

81. the razor's _____

82. rogues' _____

83. runner's _____

84. scout's _____

85. wolf in sheep's _____

86. shepherd's _____

87. squatter's _____

88. a stone's _____

89. teacher's _____

90. widow's _____

91. widow's _____

92. widow's _____

93. at wit's _____

94. woman's _____

95. woman's _____

96. the women's _____

97. worker's _____

98. writer's _____

99. writer's _____

100. a young man's _____

Each item in the next cluster starts with a person's name. For each blank, supply the proper noun that precedes each given noun, as in *Frankenstein's* monster. Remember that Frankenstein refers to the doctor, not the Boris Karloff character. Old Zipperneck is properly referred to as Frankenstein's monster.

101. _____'s Alamanack

102. _____'s ark

103. _____'s bad boy

104. all around _____'s barn

105. _____'s belt

106. _____'s Bluff

107. _____'s bosom

108. _____'s box
109. _____'s cave
110. _____'s choice
111. _____'s Code
112. _____'s Comet
113. _____'s comforters
114. _____'s cow
115. _____'s Cube
116. _____'s Dance
117. _____'s Disease
118. _____'s fables
119. _____'s Ferry
120. _____'s Follies
121. _____'s folly
122. _____' heel/tendon
123. _____'s helpers/reindeer
124. _____'s lace
125. _____'s ladder
126. _____'s lamp
127. _____'s Last Stand
128. _____'s Law
129. _____'s Locker
130. _____'s Mother
131. _____'s Needle
132. _____'s number
133. _____'s Palsy
134. _____'s Peak
135. _____'s Principle

136. _____'s razor

137. _____'s Readers

138. _____'s Rebellion

139. _____'s Revenge

140. _____'s ride

141. _____'s Rules of Order

142. for _____'s sake

143. _____'s Syndrome

144. _____'s Theory of Relativity

145. _____'s Thesaurus

146. _____'s Tomb

147. _____'s Tour

148. _____'s Vineyard

149. _____'s warts

150. _____'s wife

Here is a bonus section for book lovers. The titles of many works of literature also adhere to the *whose what* pattern. Fill in the fifteen names that kick off each literary title here, as in *Gray's* Elegy:

151. _____'s *Adventures in Wonderland*

152. _____'s *Baby*

153. _____'s *Body*

154. _____'s *Cabin*

155. _____'s *Choice*

156. _____'s *Complaint*

157. _____'s *End*

158. _____'s *Last Tape*

159. _____'s *Lives*
160. _____'s *Lover*
161. _____'s *Progress*
162. _____'s *Travels*
163. _____'s *Wake*
164. _____'s *Way*
165. _____'s *Web*

(Answers on page 124)

♦ FABULOUS FABLES*

One hot summer's day a Fox was strolling through an orchard till he came to a bunch of Grapes just ripening on a vine which had been trained over a lofty branch. "Just the thing to quench my thirst," quoth he. Drawing back a few paces, he took a run and a jump, and just missed the bunch. Turning round again with a One, Two, Three, he jumped up, but with no greater success. Again and again he tried after the tempting morsel, but at last had to give up, and walked away with his nose in the air, saying: "I am sure they are sour."

And that is why even today, when people disparage something that is beyond their reach, we say that their attitude is one of "sour grapes."

The Lion went once a-hunting along with the Fox, the Jackal, and the Wolf. They hunted and they hunted till at last they surprised a Stag, and soon took its life. Then came the question how the spoil should be divided. "Quarter me this Stag," roared the Lion; so the other animals skinned it and cut it into four parts. Then the Lion took his stand in front of the carcass and pronounced judgment: "The first quarter is for me in my capacity as King of Beasts; the second is mine as arbiter; another share comes to me for my part in the chase; and as for the fourth quarter, well, as for that, I should like to see which of you will dare to lay a paw upon it."

Now you know the origin of the common expression the "lion's share," which has changed meaning since its first telling. In the original story "the lion's share" meant

---

*The fables in this chapter are retellings by Joseph Jacobs in *The Fables of Aesop* (New York: Macmillan, 1964).

all of something—the whole shebang, ball of wax, and shootin' match. Nowadays the phrase means a portion larger than anyone else's.

One of the richest veins from which nuggets of verbal wisdom are mined is the fable, a made-up story that often involves talking animals. In olden days such tales were described as "fablelike," or fabulous. By a process that linguists call generalization, anything that is wonderful, astonishing, or delightful has come to be called "fabulous." The stories of "The Fox and the Grapes" and "The Lion's Share" are associated with the legendary fabulist Aesop. We don't know much about Aesop, but he is said to have lived in the middle of the sixth century B.C. and been the black slave of a Thracian in Greece. According to tradition, Aesop was deformed and ugly and used fables to bolster his arguments and, ultimately, to win his freedom.

Fables have made many fabulous contributions to the English language. Here are brief versions of seven of Aesop's fables, each of which has bequeathed us a familiar phrase or saying. The nugget of wisdom may come from the story itself or from the moral, which, in each case, I have omitted. Identify each expression:

1. A Wolf found great difficulty in getting at the sheep owing to the vigilance of the shepherd and his dogs. But one day it found the skin of a sheep that had been flayed and thrown aside, so it put it on over its own pelt and strolled among the sheep.

2. A Hare and a Tortoise agreed to have a footrace. The Hare darted almost out of sight at once, but soon stopped and, to show his contempt for the Tortoise, lay down to have a nap. The Tortoise plodded on and on, and when the Hare awoke from his nap, he saw the Tortoise just near the winning post and could not run up in time to save the race.

a wolf in sheep's clothing

3. One day a countryman going to the nest of his Goose found there an egg of pure gold. Every morning the same thing occurred, and he grew rich by selling his eggs. As he grew rich he grew greedy; and thinking to get at once all the gold the Goose could give, he killed it and opened it only to find—nothing.

4. A Waggoner was once driving a heavy load along a very muddy way. At last he came to a part of the road where the wheels sank halfway into the mire, and the more the horses pulled, the deeper sank the wheels. So the Waggoner threw down his whip, and knelt down and prayed to Hercules the Strong: "O Hercules, help me in my hour of distress," quoth he.

But Hercules appeared to him and said: "Tut, man, don't sprawl there. Get up and _____."

5. Long ago, the mice held a general council to consider what measures they could take to outwit their common enemy, the Cat. Some said this, and some said that; but at last a young mouse got up and said: "I propose that a small bell be procured, and attached by a ribbon around the neck of the Cat. By this means we should always know when she was in the neighborhood."

The proposal met with general applause, until an old mouse got up and said: "That's all very well, but who is to _____?" The mice looked around at one another, and nobody spoke.

6. A Man had lost his way in a wood one bitter winter's night. As he was roaming about, a Satyr came up to him and promised to give him lodging for the night. As he went along to the Satyr's cell, the Man raised both his hands to his mouth and kept on blowing at them. "What do you do that for?" asked the Satyr.

"My hands are numb with the cold," said the Man, "and my breath warms them."

After this they arrived at the Satyr's home, and soon the Satyr put a smoking dish of porridge before him. But when the Man raised his spoon to his mouth he began blowing upon it. "And what do you do that for?" said the Satyr.

"The porridge is too hot, and my breath will cool it."

"Out you go," said the Satyr. "I will have nought to do with a man who can _____ with the same breath."

7. A Dog looking out for its afternoon nap jumped into the Manger of an Ox and lay there cosily upon the straw. But soon the Ox, returning from its afternoon of work, came up to the manger and wanted to eat some of the straw. The Dog in a rage, being awakened from its slumber, stood up and barked at the ox, and whenever it came near attempted to bite it. At last the ox gave up the hope of getting the straw and went away.

(Answers on page 126)

♦ Familiar Misquotations

Whenever a phrase or sentence becomes part of the common language, there is a strong possibility that it will be quoted inaccurately. As with all kinds of long-distance communication, the original message gets slightly garbled. Over the course of time, a letter is shifted or a word is changed, and forevermore the quotation becomes a cliché that nobody ever gets quite right.

Early in this century the columnist and wit Franklin P. Adams devised a quiz to make us feel like idiots. Here are four items from that quiz:

- From "The Rime of the Ancient Mariner," complete the statement "Water, water everywhere . . ."
- What words follow "Alas, poor Yorick"?
- What grow "from little acorns"?
- Finish the line " 'Twas the night before Christmas . . ."

The answers:

- "Nor any drop to drink" (usually misquoted "and not a drop to drink")—Samuel Taylor Coleridge
- "I knew him, Horatio" (usually "I knew him well")—William Shakespeare
- "Tall oaks" (Alas, poor reader. It's not "great oaks")—David Everett
- "While all through the house" (generally "and

all through the house")—Clement Clarke Moore

If you got all four items right, you are blessed with an encyclopedic mind, a photographic memory, and a phonographic ear. I am also immensely jealous of you and dismiss you from playing the following game. But don't go off too fully cocked. Remember that "a little knowledge is a dangerous thing."

Even better, remember that—in the mortal words of Alexander Pope—"a little learning is a dangerous thing."

If you are reasonably normal and missed all four questions, I invite you to try out some more old saws and see how badly you get cut. Complete each proverbial cliché:

1. "_____ is the root of all evil."—I Timothy
2. "A penny for your _____."
—John Heywood
3. "Till death _____ part."
—wedding vow
4. "_____ will have his day."
—William Shakespeare
5. "Play it, _____."—Humphrey Bogart, as Rick in *Casablanca*
6. "I have nothing to offer but blood, _____."
—Winston Churchill
7. "Give him an inch, he'll take _____."
—John Ray
8. "Variety is the _____ of life."
—William Cowper
9. "_____ the skin of my teeth."—Job
10. "Music hath charms to soothe _____."
—William Congreve

11. "To _____ the lily."—William Shakespeare
12. "Under _____ spreading chestnut tree/The village smithy stands."—Henry Wadsworth Longfellow
13. "Pride goeth before _____."—Proverbs
14. "One good turn _____ another."—John Heywood
15. "Ask me no questions, and I'll tell you no _____."—Isaac Watts
16. "Imitation is the sincerest _____."—Walter Colton
17. "All that _____ is not gold."—William Shakespeare
18. "_____ is the gate and narrow is the way."—Matthew
19. "Beggars _____ choosers."—Beaumont and Fletcher
20. "Better halfe a loafe than _____."—William Camden
21. "Went in _____ ear and out _____."—John Heywood
22. "All I know is what I _____ in the papers."—Will Rogers
23. "Sticks and stones may break my bones/But _____ can never _____."—Old English rhyme
24. "_____ not to reason why/_____ but to do and die."—Alfred Lord Tennyson
25. "Birds of a feather _____ together."—Robert Burton
26. "I only regret that I have but one life to _____ for my country."—Nathan Hale

27. "And one man in his _____
    plays many parts."—William Shakespeare
28. "To the _____ born."—William Shakespeare
29. "_____ better part of _____."
    —William Shakespeare
30. "Winning isn't everything, _____."
    —Vince Lombardi

(Answers on page 126)

◆ Answers

Cut and Dried Clichés

(page 79)

1. Hoyle **2.** shadow **3.** the shouting **4.** the switch
5. grind **6.** woods **7.** compliment **8.** basics **9.** question
10. never

11. a hard place **12.** disguise **13.** pit **14.** mouth **15.** for
the trees **16.** sin **17.** the old block **18.** absence **19.** in the
rough **20.** conscience

21. starts **22.** purposes **23.** conclusion **24.** bear it
25. fist **26.** gone tomorrow **27.** and cry **28.** an eye
29. effort **30.** on life

31. my mind **32.** meet **33.** main **34.** truth **35.** ends
36. simple **37.** wiser **38.** so good **39.** image **40.** in a round
hole

41. mad **42.** scratch **43.** leave it **44.** true **45.** gauntlet
46. done **47.** wax **48.** thinking **49.** frazzle **50.** havoc

Trite as a Cliché

(page 83)

1. a coot **2.** a bat **3.** a lion **4.** a beaver **5.** a bee **6.** a
hound's tooth **7.** a bedbug **8.** a coot **9.** a loon **10.** a bear

11. a bug's ear **12.** a skunk **13.** an ox **14.** a pig **15.** a
bird **16.** a lamb **17.** an ape **18.** a lark (or clam) **19.** a pig in
spit **20.** a horse

21. a horse **22.** a goose **23.** a hornet **24.** a wet hen

25. a jaybird **26.** a kitten **27.** a partridge **28.** a churchmouse **29.** a peacock **30.** a mouse

31. a lobster **32.** hens' teeth **33.** a dog **34.** a goose **35.** an eel **36.** a fox **37.** a bug in a rug **38.** a bull **39.** an ox **40.** a mule **41.** a tick **42.** an owl **43.** all outdoors **44.** mud **45.** ice **46.** falling off a log **47.** lightning **48.** a daisy **49.** gold **50.** grass **51.** a rock **52.** blazes **53.** a feather **54.** the hills **55.** the driven snow **56.** rain **57.** a rock, the Rock of Gibraltar **58.** an oak

59. apple pie **60.** a berry **61.** a cucumber **62.** pie **63.** a pancake **64.** a fruitcake **65.** a beet **66.** molasses (in January) **67.** butter **68.** honey **69.** sugar **70.** pea soup **71.** toast **72.** a prune

73. a billiard ball **74.** a house **75.** the ace of spades **76.** pitch **77.** an old shoe **78.** a button **79.** a doornail **80.** a post

81. dust **82.** dishwater (actually ditchwater) **83.** a crutch **84.** a kite **85.** an oven **86.** a dishrag **87.** a pin **88.** a ghost **89.** a picture **90.** sandpaper

91. a tack **92.** silk **93.** a board **94.** velvet **95.** a toothpick **96.** a drum **97.** a spring **98.** nails **99.** shoe leather **100.** a sheet

101. straight **102.** clear **103.** dry **104.** rich **105.** plain **106.** honest **107.** naked **108.** odd **109.** sound **110.** fit

111. quick **112.** mad **113.** sober **114.** big **115.** drunk **116.** old **117.** innocent **118.** different **119.** plain **120.** hot

121. thin **122.** sure **123.** ugly **124.** thick **125.** phony **126.** silent **127.** clean **128.** quick

AVOID CLICHÉS LIKE THE PLAGUE

(page 93)

1. a balloon **2.** a battleship **3.** a brick spithouse **4.** a rose **5.** a white tornado **6.** a fox **7.** gangbusters **8.** a baby **9.** a hot potato **10.** flies

11. a bird **12.** a pig **13.** there was no tomorrow

14. looking for a needle in a haystack   15. a glove   16. new
17. getting blood from a stone (or turnip)   18. pulling teeth
19. the palm (or back) of my hand   20. Topsy

21. a weed   22. a hole in the head   23. a ton of bricks
24. a rug   25. a Christmas tree   26. a king   27. a bandit   28. a
lion   29. lamb   30. butter

31. an elephant('s)   32. a sieve   33. a steel trap
34. wildfire   35. water off a duck's back   36. a chicken with its
head cut off   37. a deer 38. the wind   39. a stone   40. hotcakes

41. a leaf   42. a million dollars   43. death warmed over
44. something the cat dragged in   45. a duck to water   46. a
baby   47. a log   48. a top   49. a chimney   50. an eagle

51. it was going out of style   52. a sore thumb   53. a thief
in the night   54. a trooper   55. ships in the night   56. two peas
in a pod   57. a duck to water   58. dirt   59. a banshee   60. a
hawk

61. clockwork   62. a broken record   63. a lead balloon
64. a charm   65. a Trojan

DYNAMIC TRIOS

(page 97)

1. ready, willing   2. God, motherhood   3. up, up   4. papa
bear, mama bear   5. lock, stock   6. eat, drink   7. baubles,
gangles   8. red, white   9. bell, book   10. faith, hope

11. baseball, apple pie   12. man, woman   13. food, shelter
14. calm, cool   15. Doric, Ionic   16. signed, sealed   17. was, is
18. here, there   19. first in peace, first in war   20. of the people,
by the people

21. solid, liquid   22. tall, dark   23. high, wide   24. fat,
dumb   25. Father, Son   26. me, myself   27. on land, on sea
28. upstairs, downstairs   29. executive, legislative   30. a hop,
skip

31. stop, look   32. gold, frankincense   33. masculine, fem-
inine   34. the truth, the whole truth   35. love, honor   36. snap,
crackle   37. princes, powers   38. life, liberty   39. readin', 'ritin'
40. sex, drugs

41. shake, rattle 42. equilateral, isoceles 43. name, rank
44. hook, line 45. wine, women 46. knife, fork 47. sun,
moon 48. id, ego 49. screwed, blued 50. blood sweat (Winston Churchill actually said, "I have nothing to offer but blood,
toil, tears, and sweat.")

51. ear, nose 52. bacon, lettuce 53. *The Good, the Bad*
54. *The Lion, the Witch* 55. hither, thither

56. lights! camera! 57. lions, tigers 58. ifs, ands 59. the
butcher, the baker 60. a b 61. friends, Romans 62. win, lose
63. sugar, spice 64. ready! aim! 65. way, shape 66. liberty,
equality 67. ready! set! 68. on your mark! get set! 69. going!
going! 70. doctor, lawyer

71. good, bad 72. It's a bird! It's a plane! 73. coffee, tea
74. animal, vegetable 75. fold, spindle 76. snips, snails
77. rock, paper 78. win, place 79. rain, sleet 80. hear no
evil, see no evil

81. beg, borrow 82. wham, bam 83. person, place
84. tic tac 85. veni, vidi

86. Shadrach, Meshach 87. Porthos, Athos 88. Caspar,
Melchior 89. Tinkers, Evers 90. Flopsy, Mopsy

91. Tom, Dick 92. Manny, Moe 93. Angles, Saxons
94. Huey, Dewey 95. Peter, Paul 96. Crosby, Stills
97. Wynken, Blynken 98. Kukla, Fran 99. the Atchison, Topeka 100. the *Nina,* the *Pinta*

WHOSE WHAT?

(page 104)

1. eye view 2. eye 3. cradle 4. paw 5. meow
6. pajamas 7. whiskers 8. age 9. feet 10. nest

11. life 12. legs 13. teeth 14. nest 15. ass 16. share
17. nest 18. uncle 19. eye 20. pace

21. length 22. foot 23. breath 24. dozen 25. luck
26. buff (not bluff; *buff* is short for "buffet") 27. rush 28. lunch
29. holiday 30. proof

31. salad 32. surprise 33. play 34. arrest 35. item
36. work 37. float 38. list 39. door 40. prison
41. advocate 42. doctor 43. mustache 44. fee
45. carry 46. errand 47. gold 48. paradise 49. "C"
50. agreement
51. eye 52. breadth (not *breath*) 53. way 54. delight
55. desire 56. sake 57. Angels 58. Kitchen 59. knee
60. delight
61. Witnesses 62. ransom 63. English 64. man
65. night 66. Prayer 67. lane 68. leap 69. quarrel
70. boy
71. eye 72. helper 73. milk 74. row 75. land
76. tale 77. pants 78. field 79. wheel 80. devil
81. edge 82. gallery 83. high 84. honor 85. clothing
86. pie 87. rights 88. throw 89. pet 90. peak
91. walk 92. weeds 93. end 94. intuition 95. work
96. movement 97. compensation 98. block 99. cramp
100. fancy
101. Poor Richard 102. Noah 103. Peck 104. Robin
Hood 105. Orion 106. Coogan 107. Abraham
108. Pandora 109. Plato 110. Hobson
111. Hammurabi 112. Halley 113. Job 114. Mrs.
O'Leary 115. Rubik 116. St. Vitus 117. Alzheimer, Parkinson, etc. 118. Aesop 119. Harper 120. Ziegfeld
121. Fulton, Seward 122. Achilles 123. Santa
124. Queen Anne 125. Jacob 126. Aladdin 127. Custer
128. Boyle, Murphy, etc. 129. Davy Jones 130. Whistler
131. Cleopatra 132. Avogadro 133. Bell 134. Pike, etc.
135. Archimedes, Bernoulli, etc. 136. Ockham
137. McGuffey 138. Shays, Turner, etc. 139. Montezuma,
Ramses (depending on the country in which one is smitten)
140. Paul Revere
141. Robert (not *Roberts*) 142. Christ, Pete 143. Down,
etc. 144. Einstein 145. Roget 146. Grant 147. Cook
148. Martha 149. Planter 150. Caesar, Lot, Potiphar

151. *Alice*   **152.** *Rosemary*   **153.** *John Brown*   **154.** *Uncle Tom*
155. *Sophie*   **156.** *Portnoy*   **157.** *Howard*   **158.** *Krapp*
159. *Dubin*   **160.** *Lady Chatterley*
161. *Pilgrim*   **162.** *Gulliver*   **163.** *Finnegan*   **164.** *Swann*
165. *Charlotte*

FABULOUS FABLES

(page 112)

1. a wolf in sheep's clothing   **2.** Slow and steady wins the race.   **3.** to kill the goose that lays the golden egg   **4.** put your shoulder to the wheel   **5.** bell the cat   **6.** blow hot and cold   **7.** a dog in the manger

FAMILIAR MISQUOTATIONS

(page 117)

1. the love of money   **2.** thought   **3.** us do   **4.** Dog
5. Sam   **6.** toil, tears, and sweat   **7.** an el   **8.** very spice
9. with   **10.** a savage breast

11. paint   **12.** a   **13.** destruction   **14.** asketh   **15.** fibs
16. of flattery   **17.** glisters   **18.** strait   **19.** must be no   **20.** no bread

21. at the one . . . at the other   **22.** see   **23.** words . . . harm me   **24.** Theirs . . . theirs   **25.** will gather   **26.** lose   **27.** time
28. manner   **29.** The . . . valor is discretion   **30.** but wanting to win is

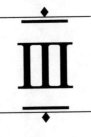

Sound

"The sound must seem an echo of the sense."

—Alexander Pope

◆ ALLITERACY

The English language abounds with alliteration—series of sequential syllables starting with the same sound. To prove my point and put my money where my mouth is, I offer the cream of the crop—a treasure trove of a hundred tried-and-true, bread-and-butter, bigger-and-better, bright-eyed-and-bushy-tailed, back-to-basics, larger-than-life, clear-cut (not haphazard and halfhearted) alliterative expressions (the more the merrier) that are good as gold, worth a pretty penny, and not a dime a dozen—guaranteed to leave you head over heels and jumping for joy to beat the band.

In each case, supply the missing word, as in "fame and *fortune*":

1. Adam's _____
2. baby _____
3. beat around the _____
4. a bee in her _____
5. bite the _____
6. black _____
7. black and _____
8. bosom _____
9. bottom of the _____
10. brains and _____
11. calm, cool, and _____
12. candid _____

13. a close _____

14. too close for _____

15. the coast is _____

16. cool _____

17. copy _____

18. a dead _____

19. defend to the _____

20. dog _____

21. down in the _____

22. dribs and _____

23. fact or _____

24. fast _____

25. fast and _____

26. feast or _____

27. few and _____

28. fish nor _____

29. fist _____

30. footloose and _____

31. friend or _____

32. gas _____

33. the gift of _____

34. head _____

35. head for _____

36. head over _____

37. hide nor _____

38. hit the _____

39. hitch _____

40. hold your _____

41. house and _____
42. kangaroo _____
43. kingdom _____
44. kit and _____
45. kith and _____
46. labor of _____
47. the last _____
48. lay of the _____
49. left in the _____
50. live and _____
51. mass _____
52. master_____
53. mince_____
54. mind over _____
55. pay the _____
56. penny wise and _____
57. pen _____
58. pet _____
59. poison _____
60. prim and _____
61. rags to _____
62. rest and _____
63. road_____
64. rock and _____
65. rough and _____
66. round _____
67. run _____
68. better safe than _____

a pet peeve

69. ship _____

70. short _____

71. side _____

72. sight _____

73. solar _____

74. stage _____

75. sure as _____

76. sweet _____

77. take your _____

78. takes its _____

79. tall _____

80. tattered and _____

81. time and _____

82. time will _____

83. tit for _____

84. toast of the _____

85. tongue _____

86. tools of the _____

87. trials and _____

88. trick or _____

89. turn the _____

90. twist and _____

91. vim and _____

92. waiting in the _____

93. wax and _____

94. wear out your _____

95. wet your _____

96. white _____

97. whole _____

98. the whys and _____

99. wild and _____

100. worth_____

(Answers on page 151)

♦ | INKY PINKY

What do you get when you dip your little finger into a bottle of writing fluid? An inky pinky.

Looking for an entertaining way to sharpen both your ear for rhyme and your skill in defining words? Try the Inky Pinky game, a favorite of mine because my three children were brought up playing endless rounds of it during long car trips. I'm convinced that all those hours of juggling sounds and definitions have made them more verbivorous adults.

In Inky Pinky, the first player offers a concise, clear definition and the second player must translate that definition into two words that rhyme. The first player must also indicate the number of syllables in each word by saying "Ink Pink" for one-syllable words, "Inky Pinky" for two-syllable words, and so on.

To warm up for the challenge, consider the following examples:

> **Definition:** an uncontrollable youngster. *Ink Pink*.
> **Answer:** a wild child.
> **Definition:** a dumb little boy with a bow and arrow. *Inky Pinky*.
> **Answer:** a stupid cupid.
> **Definition:** a yearly handbook. *Inkity Pinkity*
> **Answer:** an annual manual.

Now that the chalk talk is over, translate the following lists of definitions into rhyming pairs, using the headings

stupid cupid

as clues to the number of syllables in each word. For more fun, create your own definitions and challenge your family and friends to discover the rhymed answers:

⎯⎯⎯⎯ ◆ ⎯⎯⎯⎯

INK PINK

⎯⎯⎯⎯ ◆ ⎯⎯⎯⎯

1. inexpensive land vehicle
2. short poetry
3. strange facial hair
4. meat robber
5. large dried fruit
6. contemptible sign of happiness
7. crack in a safe
8. dock for shorties
9. pale long-necked bird
10. shining armor-wearer
11. crazy flatboat
12. intelligent pointed missile
13. bad smell in a ditch
14. bad-tempered monarch
15. wet hobo
16. porcine toupee
17. stupid finger
18. wheat-carrying vehicle
19. grass strength
20. inebriated animal

drunk as a skunk

♦

INKY PINKY

♦

21. comical hare
22. vegetable for talking bird
23. unreliable dill
24. even demon
25. fishy operating-room doctor
26. cross cat
27. gruesome tale
28. horrible couple
29. thin shaft
30. elementary skin eruption
31. indolent flower
32. strange stogie
33. drunk fortune-teller
34. strong-smelling tramp
35. basement resident
36. careful pupil
37. adroit finger-protector
38. small person's nervous habit
39. happy boat
40. doorway for guards
41. mob's chatter
42. threat on the court
43. light sprite
44. web-spinner's drink
45. nuptial land vehicle
46. superior woolen garment
47. simian textile trim
48. thrifty horn
49. herder of spotted cats
50. untippable piece of furniture

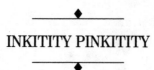

INKITY PINKITY

51. ominous clergyman
52. frozen bike
53. tantrum thrown by Cleopatra
54. pasta torn into little pieces
55. mundane pattern of tiles
56. ceatacean's soundness of mind
57. conference about a head injury
58. pessimistic mountaintop
59. display of sweets
60. horned animal's melon
61. how to save the environment
62. dead man's talk
63. elastic bushes
64. software contester
65. Hebrew walking stick

Now it's time to step up to some prodigiously poly-syllabic posers:

INKITITY PINKITITY

66. royal cloth
67. crazy leave of absence
68. floor-covering oil
69. maudlin Asian
70. self-reliant overseer

71. microscopic plants in Russia
72. bubbly teenager
73. star war
74. deafening ancient chant
75. inoperative power plant

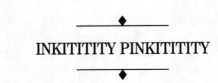

INKITITITY PINKITITITY

76. police lexicon
77. incapable scholar
78. meatless lover of things old
79. satisfaction from passing amendments
80. opinion article in tropical newspaper

(Answers on page 152)

♦ TIME FOR RHYME

In the game of Inky Pinky, the players fabricate their most creative and outrageous rhymes. But a deep richness of rhyme reposes naturally and subtly in the words and phrases that we use every day. Just as Molière's M. Jourdain was delighted to learn that he had been speaking prose his whole life, you may be surprised to discover that you have been speaking a kind of poetry throughout yours.

Open your ears now to a list of compound words and word pairs, each with the second half missing. Complete each item by supplying the missing rhyme, as in "clap-trap." *Claptrap* was originally a theatrical term for a showy trick or patch of high-flown, grandiose language that actors would use to attract (trap) applause (claps) from their audiences.

1. air _____
2. band _____
3. bar _____
4. bed _____
5. big _____
6. black _____
7. boob _____
8. dead _____
9. fat _____
10. grand _____
11. half _____

12. hand _____
13. hey _____
14. hot _____
15. low _____
16. May _____
17. night _____
18. nit _____
19. pay _____
20. pot _____
21. red _____
22. speed _____
23. spring _____
24. sure _____
25. sweet _____
26. tie _____
27. true _____
28. way _____
29. wheeler _____
30. wing _____

For the next items, supply the missing first half of each rhyme:

31. _____ away
32. _____ baloney
33. _____ bean
34. _____ bender
35. _____ book
36. _____ drain

37. _____ fi
38. _____ go
39. _____ gold
40. _____ high
41. _____ leg
42. _____ pack
43. _____ power
44. _____ pump
45. _____ scooper
46. _____ set
47. _____ share
48. _____ show
49. _____ suit
50. _____ talk
51. _____ time
52. _____ town
53. _____ track
54. _____ trouble
55. _____ will
56. _____ yokel

Now try a dozen rhymes of the "_____ and _____" variety, as in "highways and *byways*":

57. fair and _____
58. gloom and _____
59. high and _____
60. hither and _____

61. huffing and _____

62. lean and _____

63. near and _____

64. run and _____

65. slice and _____

66. town and _____

67. wear and _____

68. wine and _____

Finally, here are a number of rhyming expressions that contain more than two words. Complete each phrase by filling in the blanks, as in "by hook or by *crook*." The expression comes from the custom in feudal times of allowing peasants in need of firewood to take only those tree branches that hung low enough to be pulled down or cut off by hook or by crook:

69. ants in your _____

70. a blast from the _____

71. claim to _____

72. court of last _____

73. different _____
for different _____

74. drunk as a _____

75. fill the _____

76. go with the _____

77. haste makes _____

78. hot to _____

79. hunk of _____

80. in like _____

81. knock your _____ off
82. _____, _____,
   and barrel
83. loose as a _____
84. loose lips sink _____
85. made in the _____
86. make or _____
87. might makes _____
88. the name of the _____
89. no _____, no _____
90. no way, _____
91. pay your _____
92. pie in the _____
93. sneak a _____
94. son of a _____
95. sticks and _____ may break
   my _____
96. take the _____
97. walk a _____ _____
98. Your _____ is _____ .

And, of course, we must end with:

99. See you _____,
   _____ .
100. After _____,
   _____ .

(Answers on page 153)

♦ **SUPER-DUPER REDUPLICATIONS**

Very early in our careers as language users we start taking great pleasure in repeating playful sounds. In the crib and romper room we babble *ma-ma, da-da,* and *bye-bye.* Soon we are intoning such ditties as *eeny meeny miny moe, fee fi fo fum,* and *hickory dickory dock,* not because they make a lot of sense to us, but because they satisfy a primal craving for rhythm and rhyme. The appeal of such playful repetitions is especially evident in the story of Chicken Little (also known as Chicken Licken) and his friends Henny Penny, Cocky Locky, Ducky Lucky, Goosey Loosey, and Turkey Lurkey, and their nemesis Foxy Loxy.

When a sound or syllable repeats itself with little or no change in a word, the resulting combination is often a reduplication. There are more than two thousand such twin words in English, and they come in three varieties— rhymes, like *hocus-pocus;* vowel shifts, like *zigzag;* and repetitions, like *goody-goody.*

A number of rhyming reduplications have intriguing origins. The hob in *hobnob* is a projection from a fireplace used to warm drinks; the nob is a table on which the drinks are placed—an appropriate setting for hobnobbing. A *hodgepodge* (earlier *hotchpotch*) was originally a stew of many ingredients and has broadened in meaning to signify a widely varied concoction, a mess. *Willy-nilly* issues from the phrase "will I, nill I?"—*nill* being an obsolete word meaning "not to will, to refuse." Many linguists attribute *nitty-gritty* to the Black English expression "grits like nits," that is, "lice (nits) that are hard as grits."

I invite you to discover the ubiquity of reduplications in our language by playing a super-duper, handy-dandy, okey-dokey, razzle-dazzle, hotsy-totsy, tip-top game. Match each clue in the left-hand column with the appropriate reduplication, or reduplications, in the right-hand column:

RHYMES

1. a kind of radio microphone	*boogie-woogie*
2. that which is basic	*bowwow*
3. an old stick-in-the-mud	*crumbum*
4. a barrel organ	*even Stephen*
5. characterizing the rabble	*flibbertigibberty*
6. a dog's bark	*fuddy-duddy*
7. wimpy	*fuzzy-wuzzy*
8. a suggestive dance	*handy-dandy*
9. outwardly affectionate	*hanky-panky*
10. Native American tent	*heebie-jeebies*
11. Native American council	*helter-skelter, pell-mell*
12. meaningless chatter	*herky-jerky*
13. short and pudgy	*hobnob*
14. a call to gain attention	*hocus-pocus,*
15. flashy	*abracadabra*
16. useful and wonderful	*hoi polloi, ragtag*
17. an equal split	*hoity-toity*
18. magician's incantation	*hokey-pokey*
19. a type of blues music	*hootchy-kootchy,*
20. in close friendship	*fan-tan*
21. furry	*hugger-mugger*
22. a confused state	*humdrum*
	hurdy-gurdy

23. boring, routine
24. erratic movement
25. sexual activity
26. slow
27. extreme nervousness
28. snobbish
29. to socialize
30. without plan
31. uproar, tumult
32. to keep secret
33. expression of approval
34. very small
35. frivolous, flighty
36. an unsavory character

hurly-burly,
    hustle-bustle
lovey-dovey
mumbo jumbo, folderol
namby-pamby
nitty-gritty
okeydokey,
    super-duper
palsy-walsy
powwow
razzle-dazzle,
    hotsy-totsy
roly-poly
teeny-weeny, itsy-bitsy
tepee
walkie-talkie
willy-nilly
yoo-hoo

♦

VOWEL SHIFTS

♦
---

37. sound a clock makes
38. sound a bell makes
39. sound a donkey makes
40. sound a horse makes
41. sound of little feet
42. playground apparatus
43. to make sharp turns
44. indecisive
45. the best
46. the rabble
47. a lulling rhythm

chitchat, fiddle-faddle
clipclop
crisscross
dillydally
dingdong, jingle-jangle
flimflam
flip-flop
heehaw
jimjams
knickknack
mishmash

48. to procrastinate

49. traverse from two directions

50. idle talk

51. a reversal of movement

52. a confused state

53. deception, fraud

54. delirium tremens

55. to hesitate

56. rackets game

57. a small ornamental item

Ping-Pong
pitter-patter
riffraff
seesaw
shilly-shally
singsong
ticktock
tiptop
wishy-washy
zigzag

♦

REPETITIONS

♦

58. an even split

59. the land of Peter Pan

60. child's toy

61. perfect vision

62. sound a train makes

63. a drum

64. extinct bird

65. ballerina's skirt

66. someone too perfect

67. '60s dance

68. something forbidden

69. an ornamental tuft

70. high-kicking dance

can-can
choo-choo, chug-chug
dodo
fifty-fifty
_go-go_
goody-goody
never-never
_no-no_
pom-pom
tom-tom
tutu
twenty-twenty
_yo-yo_

(Answers on page 154)

♦ Answers

(page 129)

Alliteracy

1. apple   2. boom   3. bush   4. bonnet   5. bullet
6. ball, berry, belt, bird, board, book, etc.   7. blue   8. buddy
9. barrel   10. brawn

11. collected   12. camera   13. call   14. comfort
15. clear   16. cat   17. cat   18. duck   19. death
20. days, doo

21. dumps   22. drabs   23. fiction   24. food, friends
25. furious   26. famine   27. far between   28. foul   29. fight
30. fancy free

31. foe   32. guzzler   33. gab   34. honcho, hunter
35. the hills   36. heels   37. hair   38. hay   39. hiker
40. horses

41. home   42. court   43. come   44. caboodle   45. kin
46. love   47. laugh   48. land   49. lurch   50. let live

51. market, media, murderer   52. mind   53. meat
54. matter   55. piper   56. pound foolish   57. pal   58. peeve
59. pen   60. proper

61. riches   62. relaxation   63. runner   64. roll   65. ready
66. robin   67. ragged, rampant   68. sorry   69. shape
70. shrift

71. saddle, show, splitting, swipe   72. seeing, for sore eyes
73. system   74. show, struck   75. shootin'   76. sixteen
77. time   78. toll   79. tale   80. torn

151

81. tide 82. tell 83. tat 84. town 85. tied, twister
86. trade 87. tribulations 88. treat 89. tables 90. turn
91. vigor 92. wings 93. wane 94. welcome
95. whistle 96. wall, wash, water 97. hearted
98. wherefores 99. woolly 100. while

INKY PINKY

(page 135)

INK PINK: 1. cheap jeep 2. terse verse 3. weird beard
4. beef thief 5. big fig 6. vile smile 7. vault fault
8. dwarf wharf 9. wan swan 10. bright knight
11. draft raft 12. smart dart 13. trench stench
14. mean queen 15. damp tramp 16. pig wig
17. dumb thumb 18. grain train 19. lawn brawn
20. drunk skunk

INKY PINKY: 21. funny bunny 22. parrot carrot
23. fickle pickle 24. level devil 25. sturgeon surgeon
26. crabby tabby 27. gory story 28. gruesome twosome
29. narrow arrow 30. simple pimple
31. lazy daisy 32. bizarre cigar 33. tipsy gypsy
34. fragrant vagrant 35. cellar dweller 36. prudent student
37. nimble thimble 38. midget fidget 39. merry ferry
40. sentry entry
41. rabble babble 42. tennis menace 43. airy fairy
44. spider cider 45. marriage carriage 46. better sweater
47. gibbon ribbon 48. frugal bugle 49. leopard shepherd
50. stable table

INKITY PINKITY: 51. sinister minister 52. icicle bicycle
53. Egyptian conniption 54. spaghetti confetti 55. prosaic mosaic 56. manatee sanity 57. concussion discussion
58. cynical pinnacle 59. confection collection 60. antelope cantaloupe 61. pollution solution 62. cadaver palaver
63. rubbery shrubbery 64. computer disputer
65. Israeli shillelagh

INKITITY PINKITITY: 66. imperial material **67.** fanatical sabbatical **68.** linoleum petroleum **69.** sentimental Oriental **70.** independent superintendent **71.** Siberia bacteria **72.** effervescent adolescent **73.** constellation altercation **74.** stentorian Gregorian **75.** utility futility

INKITITITY PINKITITITY: 76. constabulary vocabulary **77.** ineffectual intellectual **78.** vegetarian antiquarian **79.** ratification gratification **80.** equatorial editorial

TIME FOR RHYME

(page 142)

1. fare **2.** stand **3.** car **4.** spread, stead **5.** wig **6.** jack, track **7.** tube **8.** head **9.** cat **10.** stand

11. staff **12.** stand **13.** day **14.** shot, spot **15.** blow **16.** Day **17.** flight, light **18.** wit **19.** day **20.** shot

21. head **22.** read **23.** fling **24.** cure **25.** meat **26.** die **27.** blue **28.** lay **29.** dealer **30.** ding

31. lay **32.** phony **33.** green **34.** fender **35.** cook **36.** brain **37.** hi **38.** no **39.** old, rolled **40.** sky

41. peg **42.** back, snack **43.** flower **44.** sump **45.** pooper **46.** jet **47.** fair **48.** no **49.** zoot **50.** chalk

51. prime **52.** down **53.** back, black **54.** double **55.** ill **56.** local

57. square **58.** doom **59.** dry **60.** thither **61.** puffing **62.** mean **63.** dear **64.** gun **65.** dice **66.** gown **67.** tear **68.** dine

69. pants **70.** past **71.** fame **72.** resort **73.** strokes/folks **74.** skunk **75.** bill **76.** flow **77.** waste **78.** trot **79.** junk **80.** Flynn

81. block, socks **82.** lock/stock **83.** goose **84.** ships **85.** shade **86.** break **87.** right **88.** game **89.** pain/gain **90.** José

91. way **92.** sky **93.** peek **94.** gun **95.** stones/bones **96.** cake **97.** fine line **98.** ass/grass **99.** later/alligator **100.** a while/crocodile

SUPER-DUPER REDUPLICATIONS

(page 147)

1. walkie-talkie   **2.** nitty-gritty   **3.** fuddy-duddy
4. hurdy-gurdy **5.** hoi   polloi,   ragtag   **6.** bowwow
7. namby-pamby **8.** hootchy-kootchy, fan-tan **9.** lovey-dovey
10. tepee

11. powwow **12.** mumbo jumbo, folderol **13.** roly-poly
14. yoo-hoo **15.** razzle-dazzle, hotsy-totsy **16.** handy-dandy
17. even Stephen **18.** hocus-pocus, abracadabra **19.** boogie-
woogie **20.** palsy-walsy

21. fuzzy-wuzzy **22.** helter-skelter,   pell-mell **23.** hum
drum **24.** herky-jerky **25.** hanky-panky **26.** hokey-pokey
27. heebie-jeebies   **28.** hoity-toity   **29.** hobnob
30. willy-nilly

31. hurly-burly,   hustle-bustle   **32.** hugger-mugger
33. okeydokey,   super-duper **34.** teeny-weeny,   itsy-bitsy
35. flibbertigibberty **36.** crumbum

37. ticktock **38.** dingdong,   jingle-jangle   **39.** heehaw
40. clipclop **41.** pitter-patter   **42.** seesaw   **43.** zigzag
44. wishy-washy **45.** tiptop **46.** riffraff **47.** singsong

48. dillydally **49.** crisscross **50.** chitchat,   fiddle-faddle
51. flip-flop **52.** mishmash   **53.** flimflam   **54.** jimjams
55. shilly-shally **56.** Ping-Pong **57.** knickknack

58. fifty-fifty **59.** never-never **60.** yo-yo **61.** twenty-
twenty **62.** choo-choo, chug-chug **63.** tom-tom **64.** dodo
65. tutu **66.** goody-goody   **67.** go-go   **68.** no-no
69. pom-pom **70.** can-can

IV

NAMES

"There is everything in a name. A rose by any other name would smell as sweet, but would not cost as much during the winter months."

—GEORGE ADE

We all know that a bunch of sheep crowded together is a flock, that a group of antelope loping together is a herd, and that a crowd of bees buzzing together is a swarm. But have you ever heard of a cowardice of curs, a labor of moles, a cete of badgers, a covert of coots, a flush of mallards, a kindle of kittens, or a drove of kine? Most of these collective nouns evolved during the Middle Ages, when the sophisticated art of hunting demanded an equally sophisticated vocabulary to name the objects of the chase. Here's your chance to play groupie. Match the collections in the left-hand column with the animals they describe in the right-hand column:

1. a *barren* of	ants
2. a *bed* of	bears
3. a *colony* of	clams
4. a *crash* of	ducks
5. a *gaggle* of	fish
6. a *leap* of	foxes
7. an *ostentation* of	geese
8. a *paddling* of	leopards
9. a *parliament* of	lions
10. a *plague* of	locusts
11. a *pride* of	monkeys
12. a *school* of	mules
13. a *skulk* of	owls
14. a *sloth* of	peacocks
15. a *troop* of	rhinoceroses

a parliament of owls

a school of fish

Now that you're feeling confident about your mastery of animal aggregations, see how you do with thirty more group nouns of the elegantly esoteric variety:

16.	a *business* of	apes
17.	a *cast* of	boars
18.	a *charm* of	cats
19.	a *clowder* of	crows
20.	a *congregation* of	doves
21.	a *convocation* of	eagles
22.	a *covey* of	ferrets
23.	a *descent* of	finches
24.	a *dray* of	frogs
25.	a *exaltation* of	goats
26.	a *gam* of	hawks
27.	a *knot* of	herons
28.	a *murder* of	larks
29.	a *murmuration* of	magpies
30.	a *mustering* of	martens
31.	a *nye* of	nightingales
32.	a *piteousness* of	pheasants
33.	a *plump* of	plovers
34.	a *pod* of	quails
35.	a *rafter* of	ravens
36.	a *richness* of	seals
37.	a *route* of	squirrels
38.	a *siege* of	starlings
39.	a *shrewdness* of	storks
40.	a *singular* of	swine
41.	a *sounder* of	turkeys
42.	a *tidings* of	whales
43.	a *trip* of	wildfowl
44.	an *unkindness* of	wolves
45.	a *watch* of	woodpeckers

For fun, you can make up your own collective nouns for animals or for people—a prickle of porcupines, an aroma of skunks, a rash of dermatologists, a brace of orthodontists.

Moving from one beastly game to another, match each animal in the left-hand column with the appropriate adjective in the right-hand column. You know that something catlike is *feline* and something doglike is *canine*. But how elegant is your semantic sophistication in dealing with the following creatures?:

46. alligator	*apian*
47. ape	*aquiline*
48. ass	*asinine*
49. bear	*avian*
50. bee	*batrachian*
51. bird	*bovine*
52. bull	*caprine*
53. cow	*cervine*
54. deer	*diapsidian*
55. dinosaur	*draconic*
56. dragon	*elephantine*
57. eagle	*equine*
58. elephant	*eusuchian*
59. fish	*leonine*
60. fox	*lupine*
61. frog	*murine*
62. goat	*musine*
63. horse	*ovine*
64. lion	*piscine*
65. mouse	*porcine*
66. pig	*ranine*
67. rat	*simian*
68. sheep	*taurine*
69. toad	*ursine*
70. wolf	*vulpine*

Now test your knowledge of family ties between the sexes of the animal world. Cows mate with bulls and hens with roosters, naturally. Can you match the animal he's in the left-hand column with the animal she's to their right?:

71.	billy goat	*dam*
72.	boar	*duck*
73.	drake	*ewe*
74.	fox	*goose*
75.	gander	*jenny*
76.	jack	*mare*
77.	peacock	*nanny goat*
78.	ram	*peahen*
79.	sire	*sow*
80.	stallion	*vixen*

When male and female beasties mate, the product is likely to be little beasties. You know that cats make kittens, dogs puppies, cows calves, ducks ducklings, eagles eaglets, rabbits bunnies, lions cubs, and sheep lambs. Now match the zoological parents in the left-hand column with their offspring:

81.	beaver	*brit*
82.	bird	*cheeper*
83.	deer	*cygnet*
84.	eel	*elver*
85.	fish	*eyas*
86.	frog	*fawn*
87.	goat	*fledgling*
88.	goose	*foal*
89.	grouse	*fry*
90.	hare	*gosling*
91.	hawk	*joey*
92.	herring	*kid*

93.	horse	*kit*
94.	kangaroo	*leveret*
95.	oyster	*poult*
96.	pig	*shoat*
97.	pigeon	*smolt*
98.	salmon	*spat*
99.	swan	*squab*
100.	turkey	*tadpole*

(Answers on page 211)

♦ NAME THAT THINGAMABOB

When you were a kid, you probably played with those small winged thingamabobs that grow on—and contain the seeds of—maple trees. You may have glued them to your nose or watched them spin like pinwheels when you tossed them into the wind. Believe it or not, these organic whatchamacallits do have a name—*schizocarps.* So does the uglifying fleshy growth on a turkey's face—a *snood*—and the heavy flaps on the sides of the mouths of some dogs—*flews.* Name-givers of the past have designated the half-smoked plug of tobacco in a pipe bowl as *dottle,* the decaying matter on a forest floor as *duff,* and the slit made when one starts to saw a piece of wood as the *kerf.*

Ever since Adam assigned names to all the animals, we human beings have managed to come up with labels for almost everything on this planet—and beyond. Many of these names are so obscure that no one except dictionary editors knows them. The rest of us are reduced to referring to these things with words that mean "that object I don't know the name for." According to *Roget's Thesaurus,* there are at least thirty ways of doing this:

dingus	*doodad*	*hootenanny*
dofunny	*dowhackey*	*hootmalalie*
dohickey	*flumadiddle*	*jigger*
dojigger	*gigamaree*	*such-and-such*
dojiggy	*gimmick*	*thingum*
domajig	*gizmo*	*thingumabob*
domajigger	*hickey*	*thingamabob*

thingamadoddle	*thingammaree*	*whatchamacallit*
thingamajig	*thingammy*	*whatzit*
thingamajigger	*whatchy*	*widget*

Here are descriptions of thirty dohickeys—things that are all around you that you probably never knew had names. The first cluster consists of items of hardware. Match each description with its label:

1. the shaft on the top of an umbrella
2. the metal hoop that supports a lampshade
3. the two buttons a telephone receiver rests on
4. the vertical post that runs through a door hinge
5. the little plastic tip of a shoelace
6. the rim of a barrel
7. the wire handle of a bucket
8. the decorative metal plate around a keyhole, drawer pull, or doorknob
9. the open-sided box in which a book is kept
10. the thin end of a knife blade that fits into the handle
11. the pointy, curved end of a wooden knife handle
12. the loop on the front part of a belt that secures the tip
13. the ornamental piece that screws into the top of a lamp to help secure the shade
14. the curved end on a suit hanger that forms a small loop

aglet

bail

bobeche

bollard

chimb

escutcheon

ferrule

finial

forel

harp

keeper

muntins

neb

paper bail

pintel

plungers

tang

15. the holder for a paper cone coffee cup

16. the narrowest part of an hourglass

17. the bar that holds typewriter paper in place

18. the circular wax-catcher that fits over a candle

19. the dock post that a boat is tied to

20. the frames for holding windowpanes

turnback

waist

zarf

Now match each part of the body with its proper but little-known name:

21. the thin muscle under the tongue

22. the wax that accumulates in the ear

23. the back of the hand, opposite the palm

24. the slender bone separating the nostrils

25. the vertical indentation that runs just below the nose to the middle of the upper lip

26. the thing that hangs down from the back of the mouth

27. the point at either end of each eye where the upper and lower lids meet

28. the fleshy bump of the ear between the side of the face and the ear cavity

29. the fleshy pad just below the thumb

30. the hollow area at the back of the knee

canthus

cerumen

frenulum

opisthenar

philtrum

popliteal

thenar

tragus

uvula

vomer

(Answers on page 212)

♦ ## FEAR OF PHOBIAS

Do you have an undomesticated pet phobia? No? Think again. Does your stomach want to scream when it and you arrive at the zenith of a Ferris wheel? Does your head retract turtlelike into your body when the lightning flashes and the thunder cracks? Does the sight of a snake or a spider, or a cat or a dog send your mind into a spin cycle?

Such fears are called phobias, and there is a name for practically every one of them. Phobos, "fear," was the son of Ares, the god of war, and was the nephew of Eris, goddess of discord, and brother to Deimos, "terror." The names of our deepest dreads generally include the Greek root *phobia,* meaning "fear or hatred," affixed to another root, which is usually Greek as well.

In the left-hand column of the quiz that follows are some of humankind's most persistent fears and terrors. In the right-hand column are the names we have assigned to these things that go bump in our minds. Match each description with its proper label:

_____ ♦ _____

FEAR OF ANIMALS

_____ ♦ _____

1. fear of bees   *aelurophobia*
2. fear of bulls   *apiophobia*
3. fear of cats   *arachnephobia*
4. fear of dogs   *batarachophobia*

5. fear of frogs and toads   *cynophobia*
6. fear of horses   *galeophobia*
7. fear of mice   *herpetophobia*
8. fear of reptiles   *hippophobia*
9. fear of sharks   *musophobia*
10. fear of spiders   *taurophobia*

♦

FEARS OF NATURE

♦

11. fear of comets   *acousticophobia*
12. fear of darkness   *aquaphobia*
13. fear of electricity   *astraphobia*
14. fear of fire   *cometophobia*
15. fear of heat   *elektrophobia*
16. fear of light   *heliophobia*
17. fear of lightning   *nyktophobia*
18. fear of noise   *photophobia*
19. fear of the sun   *pyrophobia*
20. fear of water   *thermophobia*

♦

PSYCHOLOGICAL FEARS

♦

21. fear of being alone   *acrophobia*
22. fear of being dirty   *agoraphobia*
23. fear of being shot   *algophobia*
24. fear of blood   *automysophobia*
25. fear of computers   *ballistrophobia*
26. fear of crowds   *bathophobia*

27.	fear of depths	*bogyphobia*
28.	fear of drugs	*cardiophobia*
29.	fear of dying	*chronophobia*
30.	fear of enclosed spaces	*claustrophobia*
31.	fear of friendships	*cremnophobia*
32.	fear of glass	*crystallophobia*
33.	fear of goblins, demons	*demophobia*
34.	fear of growing old	*emetophobia*
35.	fear of heart disease	*erotophobia*
36.	fear of heights	*gamophobia*
37.	fear of hell	*gerasophobia*
38.	fear of marriage	*glassophobia*
39.	fear of the number thirteen	*hematophobia*
40.	fear of open spaces	*logizomechanicophobia*
41.	fear of pain	*monophobia*
42.	fear of precipices	*olfactophobia*
43.	fear of sexual feelings	*pharmacophobia*
44.	fear of smells	*scriptophobia*
45.	fear of speed	*sociophobia*
46.	fear of speaking in public	*stygiophobia*
47.	fear of time	*tacophobia*
48.	fear of vomiting	*thanatophobia*
49.	fear of words	*triskaidecaphobia*
50.	fear of writing	*verbaphobia*

(Answers on page 212)

♦ AN ANTHOLOGY OF OLOGIES

An etymologist has been defined as someone who knows the difference between etymology and entomology.

The Greek root *etymon* means "true, original," and the Greek ending *-logia* means "science or study." Thus, etymology is the science or study of true and original word meanings. And when you know that *entomon* is Greek for "insect," you can easily deduce that an entomologist studies the physical makeup and behavior of insects. Once a moth flew into a computer and destroyed a program. Because a flaw in a computer is called "a bug," we have here a fortuitous convergence of entomology and etymology.

To label various fields of study, the English language has borrowed many roots from Greek and Latin. Sociology, for example, is the study of human societies. Zoology, for another example, is the study of animals.

In the left-hand column are fifty *-ologies*. In the right-hand column are brief definitions of these disciplines. Match each label with its definition:

1. archaeology	birds
2. anthropology	contagious diseases
3. astrology	drugs
4. audiology	the earth's crust
5. biology	earthquakes
6. cardiology	embryos
7. demonology	evil spirits
8. dermatology	God

9.	ecology	handwriting
10.	embryology	hearing
11.	epidemiology	the heart
12.	ethnology	human customs
13.	gemology	human races
14.	genealogy	the influence of planets on life
15.	geology	life
16.	graphology	mind, emotions, behavior
17.	meteorology	the nervous system
18.	neurology	one's ancestors
19.	ornithology	organisms and environments
20.	penology	the past through its artifacts
21.	pharmacology	poisons
22.	psychology	precious stones
23.	seismology	prisons
24.	theology	skin
25.	toxicology	weather

Now that you're feeling secure as an ologyologist, step up to some hundred-dollar words, like *phrenology*, the study of contours of the head, and *oology*, the study of birds' eggs:

26.	arachneology	activities of organisms
27.	cetology	aging
28.	coprology	ancient documents
29.	cytology	ants
30.	epistemology	beards
31.	gerontology	bones
32.	herpetology	cells
33.	histology	the ear
34.	ichthyology	existence
35.	kinesiology	fish
36.	laryngology	fossils
37.	logology	fungi

38.	mycology	human movement
39.	myrmecology	knowledge
40.	oenology	literature and words
41.	ontology	living tissue
42.	osteology	pornography
43.	otology	reptiles
44.	paleontology	rocks
45.	papyrology	spiders
46.	petrology	symbols
47.	philology	the throat
48.	physiology	whales
49.	pogonology	wine
50.	typology	word patterns

(Answers on page 213)

◆ FICTIONARY

One of the most amusing and instructive of party games is Fictionary, a verbal competition that illustrates vividly the human passion to name everything in sight. A group of players takes turns passing around a dictionary. (A reputable, up-to-date desk dictionary is best.) The person with the dictionary chooses and announces an unusual word. If any other player knows what the word means, he or she speaks up, and another word is selected. While the dictionary keeper writes a version of the real meaning of the word on a piece of paper, all the other players fabricate phony definitions on their slips of paper. The definitions are then passed to the dictionary announcer, who shuffles them in with the real definition and reads all the entries aloud, trying to keep a straight face.

Each player gets to be the dictionary holder, and the number of rounds equals the number of participants. In each round, players receive one point for guessing the correct definition and one point for each opponent who votes for the definition they fabricated. The dictionary holder receives one point if nobody identifies the authentic definition and one point for reading the answers aloud without laughing.

As a warm-up to your playing this game at home, I offer a dozen real words from various desk dictionaries. Each word is followed by four definitions, three of which are bogus and one of which is genuine. Can you separate the whole-grain definitions from the chaff?:

1. *alpenglow*
    a. a cheap and dangerous substitute for kerosene
    b. the healthful result of eating dogfood
    c. a reddish aureate seen at sunset on a summit
    d. a bald-headed citizen of Switzerland
2. *bagette*
    a. a long, rectangular gem
    b. a Scottish musical instrument
    c. a homeless old woman
    d. a small cover for the back or arms of a chair
3. *claymore*
    a. a musical instrument of the lute family
    b. a club used for pounding Silly Putty
    c. a benign tumor
    d. a large two-edged sword
4. *defenestrate*
    a. to evacuate an army from a swamp
    b. to drive danger away
    c. to give off glitter or sparkles
    d. to throw a person or object out the window
5. *foozle*
    a. a bungling golf stroke
    b. a nozzle used to spray insecticide from a hose
    c. an instrument to shear sheep partially, for decorative effect
    d. a small stick used by teachers to point to specific letters or numbers
6. *guano*
    a. a large fan used by attendants of a sultan
    b. bird excrement, often used as fertilizer

    c. lint that accumulates inside the belly button

    d. a sash worn by gauchos of the South American pampas

7. *inquiline*

    a. falsely appearing to look like an eagle

    b. characteristic of various colorless proteins

    c. an animal that habitually lives in the abode of another species

    d. a question asked over the telephone

8. *kludge*

    a. a badly functioning computer system

    b. a thick substance that clogs motors

    c. a unit of mass equaling one liter at standard temperature

    d. a thick chocolaty confection

9. *mizzle*

    a. a gathering of feminists

    b. a flint shaped by nature

    c. to fry in a skillet

    d. to rain very fine drops

10. *nabob*

    a. a small rufflike ornament used on furniture

    b. a refusal of a request by someone named Robert

    c. a person of great wealth or prominence

    d. an unattractive hairstyle

11. *polymath*

    a. a many-sided geometric shape

    b. one of encyclopedic learning

    c. a parrot skilled in reciting numbers

    d. a catastrophic aftermath

12. *roorback*

    a. a graceful and swift African and Asian antelope

b. a bellowing exchange among lions
c. a primitive ritual marked by animal sacrifice
d. a defamatory falsehood published for political effect

(Answers on page 213)

◆ ## WHAT'S IN A NAME?

In *Romeo and Juliet,* our young heroine declaims the famous lines "What's in a name? that which we call a rose/By any other name would smell as sweet." By the end of the play we know that Juliet was wrong: The fact that her name is Capulet and Romeo's is Montague has an enormous effect on the action of the tragedy and leads to the deaths of the two star-crossed lovers.

Would a rose by any other name really smell as sweet? Many linguists would contend that a rose by another name would smell like a petunia—or a stinkweed. What's in a name? A great deal, as anyone who has ever been stuck with an odd name or cruel nickname will tell you. A number of reputable studies have shown that psychosis and criminal behavior are more common among people with "peculiar names" and that people with last names beginning with the letters *S* through *Z* die sooner than others—perhaps because they spend more of their lives tensely waiting in lines.

Hollywood's star-makers capitalize on the fact that people react emotionally to names. A star's name must have "box-office appeal"; it must project the kind of image that the star is supposed to radiate.

Would W. C. Fields have been as funny if he had retained his original name—William Claude Dukenfield—or Doris Day as popular if she had kept hers—Doris von Kappelhoff? Did Marion Michael Morrison's image become more macho when his studio changed his name to John Wayne? Here is a star-studded list of the names behind the names of some of our most celebrated celebrities.

Match each birth-certificate name in the left-hand column with its marquee counterpart in the right-hand column:

1.	Israel Isidore Baline	Lauren Bacall
2.	William Beedle	Jack Benny
3.	Angeline Brown	Irving Berlin
4.	Helen Brown	Charles Bronson
5.	Charles Bunchinsky	Red Buttons
6.	James Baumgarner	Michael Caine
7.	Aaron Chwatt	Dyan Cannon
8.	Issur Danielovitch	Cyd Charisse
9.	Arnold Dorsey	Cher
10.	Reginald Dwight	Tony Curtis
11.	Tula Ellice Finklea	Sandra Dee
12.	Samille Diane Friesen	Angie Dickinson
13.	Art Gelien	Kirk Douglas
14.	Greta Louisa Gustafsson	Bob Dylan
15.	Frances Gumm	Redd Foxx
16.	Natasha Gurdin	Greta Garbo
17.	Milton Hines	Judy Garland
18.	Gretchen Jung	James Garner
19.	Herbert Khaury	Cary Grant
20.	Simone Kaminker	Helen Hayes
21.	Hugh J. Krampe	William Holden
22.	Benjamin Kubelsky	Judy Holliday
23.	Cherilyn LaPierre	Rock Hudson
24.	Archibald A. Leach	Engelbert Humper-
25.	Maurice J. Micklewhite	dinck
26.	Steveland Morris	Tab Hunter
27.	Betty Joan Perske	Mick Jagger
28.	Michael Phillip	Elton John
29.	William Henry Pratt	Boris Karloff
30.	Wynette Pugh	Sophia Loren
31.	John Sanford	Hugh O'Brian
32.	Roy Scherer	Roy Rogers

WILLIAM
CLAUDE DUKENFIELD

MARION
MICHAEL MORRISON

CHERILYN LAPIERRE

the names behind the names

33. Bernard Schwartz
34. Sofia Scicolone
35. Leonard Franklin Slye
36. Richard Starkey
37. Raquel Tejada
38. Judith Tuvim
39. Robert Zimmerman
40. Alexandra Zuck

Soupy Sales
Simone Signoret
Ringo Starr
Tiny Tim
Raquel Welch
Stevie Wonder
Natalie Wood
Tammy Wynette
Loretta Young

(Answers on page 213)

♦ THE GAME IS THE NAME

One of the first things that we acquire when we enter this world is a name. We carry it everywhere as a badge of our individuality, and most of us cannot imagine life under a different sobriquet than our own. As poet James Russell Lowell wrote, "There is more force in names than most men dream of."

Lewis Carroll recognized this force when he wrote in *Through the Looking Glass:*

"My name is Alice . . ."

"It's a stupid name enough!" Humpty Dumpty interrupted impatiently. "What does it mean?"

"Must a name mean something?" Alice asked doubtfully.

"Of course it must," Humpty Dumpty said with a short laugh. "My name means the shape I am—and a good handsome shape it is, too. With a name like yours, you might be any shape, almost."

Dumpty is wrong in one respect: the name *Alice* does have a meaning; it means "truth." But the rotund egghead (soon to be an omelet) is perfectly correct when he eggs Alice on with "My name means the shape I am." Our name indeed gives us a "shape."

The pattern of naming in the English language began with single names because, when people lived together in small communities, the supply of names was large enough so that none had to be repeated in the same tribe or group. Most first names are very old. Girls have been named Mary ("star of the sea") and boys John ("gift of God") for many centuries, and these remain, despite fads, the most popular first names in English-speaking countries.

The egghead speaks about names.

As social groups grew larger, single names began popping up more often, and a system of distinguishing among people with the same first names had to be invented. Thus, villagers began to add a bit of descriptive information to the given name, and that's how we got last names, or surnames. The *sur* in the word comes from the Latin *super* and means "above and beyond."

Some of these surnames began life as descriptions of a person's coloring—Black, White, and Reid (Red); size—Small, Little, Longfellow; geography—Churchill, Rivers, York; or personal qualities—Smart, Wise, and Swift. A teetotaler might have picked up the name Drinkwater, a man of great strength Armstrong, and a loyal friend Truman.

Other names are patronymics and matronymics, family names derived from a parent or ancestor. Your name is probably one of these if it begins with *Mc, Mac, O',* or *Fitz,* all of which mean "son of," or ends with *son, sen, ov,* or *ovich.*

The largest category of surnames began as descriptions of the work people did. In the telephone directories of the world's English-speaking cities, Smith, which means "worker," is the most popular last name by a large margin over its nearest competitors, Jones and Johnson (both of which are patronymics). And it is no wonder when you consider that the village smith, who made and repaired all objects of metal, was the most important person in the community. International variations on Smith include Smythe, Schmidt, Smed, Faber, Ferrier, LeFebre, Ferraro, Kovacs, Manx, Goff, and Gough.

It is easy to trace the occupational origins of names such as Archer, Baker, Barber, Butler, Carpenter, Cook, Draper, Farmer, Forester, Gardener, Hunter, Miller, Potter, Skinner, Shepard, Tanner, Taylor, and Weaver. Other surnames are not so easily recognized but yield up their occupational origins with some thought and research. In the following game, match each last name listed in the left-hand column with the corresponding trade in the right-hand column:

1.	Bailey	arrow maker
2.	Baxter	bailiff
3.	Brewster	baker
4.	Chandler	bargeman
5.	Clark	barrel maker
6.	Cohen	beer manufacturer
7.	Collier	bricklayer
8.	Cooper, Hooper	candlemaker
9.	Crocker	carpenter
10.	Faulkner	clerk
11.	Fletcher	coal miner
12.	Hayward	doorkeeper
13.	Keeler	falconer
14.	Lardner	keeper of the cupboard
15.	Lederer	keeper of fences
16.	Mason	leather worker
17.	Porter	potter
18.	Sawyer	priest
19.	Schumacher	roofer
20.	Scully	scholar
21.	Stewart	shoemaker
21.	Thatcher	sty warden
23.	Travers	toll-bridge collector
24.	Wainwright	weaver
25.	Webster	wheel maker

(Answers on page 214)

◆ ## AUTHOR! AUTHOR! AUTHOR!

Once upon a time we had presidents named John Quincy Adams, William Henry Harrison, William Howard Taft, Franklin Delano Roosevelt, and John Fitzgerald Kennedy; joining them in the world of politics were the likes of William Lloyd Garrison and William Jennings Bryan. Not long ago lived thinkers named John Stuart Mill, Mary Baker Eddy, Alfred North Whitehead, Harry Emerson Fosdick, and Martin Luther King, Jr., and scientists named John James Audubon, Alexander Graham Bell, and Thomas Alva Edison. Through the world of the arts strode giants like Francis Scott Key, John Philip Sousa, Ralph Vaughan Williams, John Singer Sargent, Frederick Jackson Turner, James McNeill Whistler, and Frank Lloyd Wright; John Jacob Astor and William Randolph Hearst ruled the world of business.

What do all these luminaries have in common? They are all trinomials; that is, they were best known by three names. How many trinomials do you hear or read about in today's news? Very few, I suspect. Sure, a handful of triple names reaches out to mind—Jack Kent Cooke, Sandra Day O'Connor, Helen Gurley Brown, Norman Vincent Peale, Margaret Chase Smith, John Kenneth Galbraith, Alan Jay Lerner, Isaac Bashevis Singer, Mary Higgins Clark, Joyce Carol Oates, Catherine Drinker Bowen, and John Gregory Dunne. But this small band of exceptions serves only to remind us of an age gone by when to be known by three names was not considered stuffy or affected.

To gain a glimpse into an age when trinomials were

more in fashion, look at the middle names of dead poets and other writers who were best known by three names. In each case, supply the full name, as in *Samuel* Taylor *Coleridge:*

1. _____ Allan _____
2. _____ Ames _____
3. _____ Anne _____
4. _____ Arlington _____
5. _____ Babington _____
6. _____ Bailey _____
7. _____ Barrett _____
8. _____ Beecher _____
9. _____ Bernard _____
10. _____ Booth _____
11. _____ Branch _____
12. _____ Brinsley _____
13. _____ Brocton _____
14. _____ Butler _____
15. _____ Bysshe _____
16. _____ Carlos _____
17. _____ Chandler _____
18. _____ Clarke _____
19. _____ Conan _____
20. _____ Crowe _____
21. _____ Cullen _____
22. _____ David _____
23. _____ Dean _____

24. _____ Fenimore _____
25. _____ Gabriel _____
26. _____ Greenleaf _____
27. _____ Ingalls _____
28. _____ Jean _____
29. _____ Kinnan _____
30. _____ Laurence _____
31. _____ Laurence _____
32. _____ Lee _____
33. _____ Louis _____
34. _____ Makepeace _____
35. _____ Manley _____
36. _____ May _____
37. _____ Millington _____
38. _____ Neale _____
39. _____ Orne _____
40. _____ Payson _____
41. _____ Penn _____
42. _____ Peter _____
43. _____ Rice _____
44. _____ Russell _____
45. _____ St. Vincent _____
46. _____ Savage _____
47. _____ Stanley _____
48. _____ Vincent _____
49. _____ Wadsworth _____
50. _____ Waldo _____

51. _____ Ward _____
52. _____ Weldon _____
53. _____ Wendell _____
54. _____ Whitcomb _____
55. _____ Wing _____

Other writers prefer to be known by their initials rather than their full names. Take the initiative and match the writerly initials in the left-hand column with the last names in the right-hand column:

56. A. A.		*Andrews*
57. A. E.		*Auden*
58. A. J.		*Ballard*
59. C. P.		*Cronin*
60. C. S.		*Cummings*
61. D. H.		*Doctorow*
62. D. M.		*Donleavy*
63. E. B.		*DuBois*
64. e. e.		*Eliot*
65. E. L.		*Forster*
66. E. M.		*Frank Baum*
67. F.		*Henry*
68. H. G.		*Hinton*
69. H. H.		*Housman*
70. H. L.		*James*
71. H. P.		*Laing*
72. J. B.		*Lawrence*
73. J. D.		*Lewis*
74. J. G.		*Lovecraft*
75. J. P.		*Mencken*
76. J. R. R.		*Milne*
77. L.		*Munro*
78. O.		*Pearson*

79.	P. D.	*Perelman*
80.	P. G.	*Priestley*
81.	R. D.	*Pritchett*
82.	S. E.	*Salinger*
83.	S. J.	*Scott Fitzgerald*
84.	T. R.	*Snow*
85.	T. S.	*Somerset Maugham*
86.	V. C.	*Thomas*
87.	V. S.	*Tolkien*
88.	W.	*Wells*
89.	W. E. B.	*White*
90.	W. H.	*Wodehouse*

Still other writers prefer to be known by their pseudonyms (Greek "false name"), or pen names. Match each real name with the more famous literary name:

91.	Marie Henri Beyle	*Lewis Carroll*
92.	Eric Arthur Blair	*Joseph Conrad*
93.	Samuel Langhorne Clemens	*George Eliot*
94.	Charles Lutwidge Dodgson	*O. Henry*
95.	Mary Ann Evans	*James Herriot*
96.	Theodor Giesel	*George Orwell*
97.	Jósef Korzeniowski	*Saki*
98.	Hector Hugh Munro	*Dr. Seuss*
99.	William Sydney Porter	*Stendhal*
100.	James Alfred Wight	*Mark Twain*

(Answers on page 214)

The twain meet.

◆ ## IMMORTAL MORTALS

Long ago in prerevolutionary France there lived one Étienne de Silhouette, a controller general for Louis XV. Because of his fanatical zeal for raising taxes and slashing expenses and pensions, he enraged royalty and citizens alike, who ran him out of office within eight months.

At about the same time that Silhouette was sacked for his infuriating parsimony, the method of making cutouts of profile portraits by throwing the shadow of the subject on the screen captured the fancy of the Paris public. Because the process was cheap and one that cut back to absolute essentials, the man and the method became associated. Ever since, we have called shadow profiles *silhouettes*, with a lowercase *s*.

In the last few chapters you have seen how people get their names from words already in our language. Now let's consider how the genealogy works in both directions, how common words in our language are born from proper names. These words lose their reference to specific persons and become generic terms in our dictionaries; when they do, they usually shed their capital letters. Such additions to our vocabulary help our language to remain alive and growing, muscular and energetic.

The Greeks had a word for people who live on in our everyday conversations—*eponymos*, from which we derive the word *eponym*, meaning "after or upon a name." Stories of the origins of words made from people or places, real or imaginary, are among the richest and most entertaining about our language.

Cut it out!

Here is a quiz in which you are asked to identify twenty common words and the names of the immortal mortals from whom they descend. May this doozy of a challenge not turn you into a masochistic, namby-pamby dunce but rather galvanize you to new platonic heights of volcanic achievement:

1. In order to spend more uninterrupted time at the gambling tables, John Montagu, Fourth Earl of _____, ordered his servants to bring him an impromptu meal of slices of beef slapped between two slices of bread.

2. Samuel Augustus _____, a San Antonio rancher, acquired vast tracts of land and dabbled in cattle raising. When he neglected to brand the calves born into his herd, his neighbors began calling the unmarked offspring by his name. Through a process that linguists call generalization, this word has come to designate any nonconformist.

3. _____, the name of a courageous Apache warrior chief, became a battle cry for World War II paratroopers.

4. Amelia Jenks _____ was an American feminist who helped to publicize the once-fashionable puffy ladies' drawers that seemed to bloom like linen flowers.

5. Charles Cunningham _____, an Irish land agent, so enraged his tenants with his rent-collection policies that they threatened his life and property and burnt his figure in effigy. Hence, from Ireland comes the verb that means "to coerce an opponent through ostracism."

6. Franz Anton _____, a Viennese physician, attempted to treat his patients by fixing them with a piercing gaze, questioning them about their ailments, and stroking them with a wand. Today, a form of his name means to stimulate, as if by an electrical charge.

7. The Reverend William Archibald _____, once warden of New College, Oxford, set out to become a bird-watcher but instead became a word-botcher. He became renowned for his hilarious reversal of sounds and syllables, such as "You are occupewing my pie. May I sew you to another sheet?" and "Three cheers for our queer old dean."

8. Nicolas _____, a veteran soldier in the French First Republic and Empire, was ridiculed by his comrades for his excessive devotion to the defeated Napoleon. First used as a synonym for knee-jerk patriotism, his name was picked up during the 1970s by the feminist movement to signify attitudes of male supremacy.

9. A century before Elvis Presley, the handsome face of Civil War general Ambrose E. _____ was adorned by luxuriant side-whiskers sweeping down from his ears to his clean-shaven chin.

10. Dame Nellie _____, a famous Australian coloratura soprano, became so much the toast of the town that a toast was named after her, as well as a peachy dessert.

11. The Marquise de _____, mistress of King Louis XV, wore her hair swept straight up from the forehead in a style that became the rage of the women of Paris.

12. The European hotels of Swiss magnate César _____ were so swanky that his surname is now eponymously synonymous with high-class lodgings.

13. A snugly fitting body garment worn by dancers and acrobats descends from the name of Jules _____, a widely acclaimed French trapeze artist who was the first to perfect the aerial somersault.

14. A colorful plant characterized by scarlet leaves is especially popular at Christmastime. This Christmas flower takes its name from Joel R. _____,

sideburns

our first ambassador to Mexico, who introduced the plant to the United States from its native land.

15. In 1812, in an effort to sustain his party's power, Massachusetts governor Elbridge _____ divided the state into electoral districts with more regard to politics than to geographical reality. It happened that one of the Governor's manipulated districts resembled a salamander. To a drawing of the district a waggish cartoonist added a head, wings, and claws; the name of the creature was lent immediately to the shaping of electoral entities for political gain.

16. British engineer John L. _____ invented a durable material for repairing roads. We use his name for both the material and the act of applying it.

17. The sixteenth-century followers of the philosopher John _____ Scotus were sneered at meanly because they clung to their old beliefs instead of accepting the "new learning." Even though this philosopher was quite intelligent, we use part of his name to label people we think are stupid.

18. Dr. Thomas _____ of London was a self-appointed literary censor who published a diluted version of Shakespeare for family consumption. A form of his name has become synonymous with watering down art so as not to offend delicate sensibilities.

19. Luigi _____ was an Italian physiologist who stimulated sudden movement in frogs' legs by touching them with static electricity. Today a form of his name now means to stimulate into action, as if with an electrical charge.

20. Sylvester _____, an American dietary reformer, donated to our language the name of a cracker made of ground whole wheat flour.

(Answers on page 215)

◆ | A JIM-DANDY QUIZ

Now that you are becoming familiar with eponyms, it's time to get to know them on a first-name basis. First names, like last names, may also evolve into common words when they are used in a general sense. Consider the common teddy bear: While hunting in Mississippi, President Theodore Roosevelt spared the life of a bear cub. Ever since, the stuffed toys have borne the affectionate form of his first name.

Back in medieval times it was considered great sport to watch the antics of insane people in asylums such as Bedlam in London. The nicknames "Tom o'Bedlam" and "Tom's Fool" were often used for male inmates who were favorites of the gallery. *Tomfoolery* nowadays simply means "nonsense, silly behavior." Every *bobby* of London is named for Sir Robert Peel, who, as Home Secretary, established London's Metropolitan Police in 1829. The adjective *tawdry* is a clipping and joining of *(Sain)t Audrey,* the patron saint of Ely. On Saint Audrey's birthday, October 17, the English traditionally held a fair at which flashy jewelry, knickknacks, and lace were sold. Hence, showy finery came to be associated with Saint Audrey, and the adjective *tawdry* has been extended to mean anything cheap and gaudy in appearance or quality.

The statements in the quiz that follows concern words that contain parts that sound like first names. In most cases, the word actually descends from the first name given. Let's start with *Jack* words in the English language. Irish tradition tells us that a notorious drinker named Jack was too miserly for heaven and excluded from hell for tweaking the Devil with practical jokes. Until Judgment Day Jack is condemned to wander the earth with a lantern carved from a turnip. (The pumpkin with its fiery grin is an American adaptation.) And that's where we get our word *jack-o'-lantern*.

Show that you're a smart aleck by identifying more *Jack*-words. *Jack* may appear at the beginning or end of each answer:

1. This Jack is a large hare.
2. This Jack is stubborn as a mule.
3. This Jack is for the birds.
4. This Jack is beastly.
5. This Jack is a flower.
6. This Jack is sharp and cutting.
7. This Jack pops up all over.
8. This Jack is extremely versatile.
9. This Jack is a big winner.
10. This Jack can shatter concrete.
11. This Jack can hit you hard.
12. This Jack tastes good for breakfast.
13. This Jack can see the trees for the forest.
14. This Jack is a game played with straws.
15. This Jack takes the plane.
16. This Jack is strong enough to lift cars.
17. This Jack has you up its sleeves.
18. This Jack tries to sell you cheap goods.
19. This Jack gets the boot.
20. This Jack is wonderful!

Show that you're a jack-of-all-trades by identifying words that contain variations of the names *Bob*, *Tom*, *John*, *Bill*, and *Jim:*

21. This Bob is a whiz on snowy hills.
22. This Bob girls wear on their feet.

23. This Bob girls wear in their hair.
24. This Bob is a hairstyle.
25. This Bob is a short-tailed lynx.
26. This Bob is for the birds.
27. This Bob is for the birds, too.
28. This Bob is a nag.
29. This Bob is spindly.
30. This Tom is the cat's meow.
31. This Tom is a son of a gun.
32. This Tom is a Native American.
33. This Tom is a girl.
34. This Tom kids around a lot.
35. This Tom is utter nonsense.
36. This Tom keeps up the beat.
37. This John keeps us warm in winter.
38. This John is a flower.
39. This John tastes as good as flapjacks.
40. We visit this John several times a day.
41. This Bill is powerfully striking.
42. This Bill can get your goat.
43. This Bill heads for the hills.
44. This Bill plays games.
45. This Bill makes waves.
46. This Bill looks better than a million dollars.
47. This Jim loves ice cream.
48. This Jim can open safes.
49. This Jim has the jitters.
50. This Jim is wonderful!

(Answers on page 215)

♦ PUTTING WORDS IN THEIR PLACES

Somebody once defined a hamburger as "a humble immigrant hunk of meat that came to this country from Germany and soared to fame on a bun." That somebody was perfectly right. In its native land the dish was originally called "Hamburg steak," taking its name from the West German city of Hamburg.

After the Hamburg steak arrived in the United States midway through the last century with the first great wave of German immigrants, its name began to change. Ultimately the Hamburg steak dropped its capital *h,* acquired the suffix *er,* lost the *steak,* and moved from the platter to the plane between two slices of baked dough. *Violà:* a hamburger.

The adventure in word evolution didn't stop there. Somewhere along the way, speakers of English liberally interpreted *burger* to mean "sandwich made with a bun." Once *burger* became a new word part, *cheeseburger, beefburger, baconburger, fishburger, chiliburger,* and a trayful of other burgers entered the American scene and gullet. On a smaller scale, much the same adventure befell *frankfurter,* which takes its name from Frankfurt, Germany. *Furter* is now used to denote almost any kind of sandwich with protein slapped inside an elongated bun, as in *chickenfurter* and *fishfurter.*

Many years ago, cloth was imported into England from Silesea, then part of Germany. The material was of such poor quality that the English referred to it contemptuously as "that cloth from Silesea," or "Silesea cloth." Ultimately the phrase was shortened even further to "sleazy cloth," and that's how *sleazy* was fabricated as a popular adjective for "cheap and shoddy." Recently the word has spawned such offspring as *sleaze, sleazebag,* and *sleazeball.*

Like the names of people, place names have similarly enriched the English language with many common words; many cities, towns, regions, and nations have become eponymously enshrined in our dictionaries, usually as uncapitalized nouns. Often these words are the names of products associated with a particular location, and three of the most impressive categories of imports are alcoholic beverages, foods, and fabrics.

Among the most popular wines and liquors are amontillado (named for Montilla, Spain), asti (a town in northern Italy), beaujolais (a district in central France), bock beer (first produced in Einbeck, Germany), bourbon (a county in Kentucky), bourdeaux (a region of southern France), burgundy (France), carlowitz (a town in Yugoslavia), champagne (France), chianti (a mountainous region in Italy), cognac (a commune in Western France), daiquiri (a district in Cuba), gin (adopted from Geneva, Switzerland), a manhattan (New York), port (Oporto, Portugal), rum (Rome, Italy), sherry (Jerez, Spain), tokay (adapted from Tokaj in northeast Hungary), and tequila (a Mexican district).

To go with all that bubbly, on our table china (named for the country of China) may repose these foods: baloney (Bologna, Italy), brie (Brie district in France), brussels sprouts (Brussels, capital of Belgium), cantaloupe (papal villa of Cantalupo, Italy), camembert cheese (Normandy, France), cheddar cheese (Cheddar, England), cherrystone clams (Cheriton, Virginia), currants (Corinth, Greece), edam cheese (Edam, the Netherlands), java (Indonesian island of Java), lima beans (Lima, Peru), mayonnaise (from Mahon, a seaport in Minorca), parmesan cheese (Parma, an Italian commune), roquefort cheese (Roquefort,

France), sardine (the Sardinian coast), swiss cheese (Switzerland), tangerine (Tangiers, Morocco), vichyssoise (Vichy, France), welsh rabbit (Wales), and wiener (Wien, the German appelation for Vienna).

Among the textiles woven into the fabric of our language are calico (Calicut, India), cashmere (Kashmir, Iraq), cordovan (Cordoba, Spain), damask (Damascus, Syria), denim (de Nimes, France), duffel (Duffel, a town near Antwerp, Belgium), dungarees (Dhungaree, India), gauze (Gaza, Israel), jeans (Genoa, Italy), madras (Madras, India), muslin (Mosul, Iraq), paisley (Paisley, Scotland), satin (Tzu-t'ing, China), suede (French for "Sweden"), tulle (Tulle, France), and worsted, (Worsted, now Worstead, England).

These product categories only begin to illustrate the place that places have in our language. Using the following descriptions, identify ten common words and put them in their places:

1. Two-piece swimsuits are named after a Pacific atoll on which hydrogen bombs were detonated—a truly explosive and figurative word.

2. The most popular of all humorous verse forms in English hails from a county in Ireland. One theory says that Irish mercenaries used to compose verses in that form about each other and then join in a chorus of "When we get back to _____ town, 'twill be a glorious morning."

3. A word for smooth-sounding flattery derives from the name of a castle in County Cork, Ireland. An inscription on the wall of the castle proclaims that anyone brave enough to scale the wall and kiss a particular stone will be rewarded with the gift of influencing others through cajolery.

4. Nearly two-and-a-half millennia ago, a little band of ten thousand Athenians defeated a host of one hundred thousand Persians at the battle of _____.

bikini/Bikini

Pheidippides, a courageous runner, brought the news of the glorious victory to Athens, which lay twenty-six miles away.

5. Nineteenth-century sailors were sometimes drugged and then forced into service on ships plying the unpopular route from San Francisco to China. From the name of that Chinese port we get the verb that means "to secure someone's services through force."

6. A contraction of "St. Mary's of Bethlehem," a sixteenth-century London hospital for the insane, has become a word for uproar or confusion.

7. Another word for disorder—in this case a wild brawl—comes down to us from the name of a fair held in an Irish town near Dublin, infamous for its fistfights and rowdy behavior.

8. As an alternative to cumbersome tails on a formal full-dress dinner coat, a tailless dinner coat originated in an exclusive community about forty miles north of New York City. This short evening coat was an immediate sensation during the Gay Nineties; it is still obligatory at many formal functions a century later.

9. The Pilgrims found in America a wild fowl somewhat similar in appearance to a fowl they had known back in England—a bird that had acquired its name because it was first imported by way of a particular country. Because we perceive this bird as ugly in appearance and voice, we sometimes assign its name to people we don't care for.

10. The inhabitants of an ancient Greek city were noted for their ability to say a lot in a few words. During a siege of their capital, a Roman general sent a note to this city's commander warning that if the Romans captured the city, they would burn it to the ground. From within the city gates came back the terse reply: "If!" The city's name lives on in an adjective that describes spare speech.

(Answers on page 216)

♦ ## ENGLISH THROWS THE
BOOK AT US

When people misuse words in an illiterate but humorous manner, we call the result a *malapropism.* The word echoes the name of Mrs. Malaprop (from the French *mal à propos,* "not appropriate"), a character who first strode the stage in 1775 in Richard Brimsley Sheridan's comedy *The Rivals.* Mrs. Malaprop was an "old weather-beaten she dragon" who took special pride in her use of the King's English but who unfailingly mangled big words all the same: "Sure, if I reprehend anything in this world it is the use of my oracular tongue and a nice derangement of epitaphs!" She meant, of course, that if she comprehended anything, it was a nice arrangement of epithets.

In his epic poem *Paradise Lost,* John Milton invented *Pandemonium*—literally "a place for all the demons"—as the name of the home for Satan and his devilish friends. Because the devils were noisy, the meaning of *pandemonium,* now lowercased, has been broadened to mean "uproar and tumult."

The story of eponyms would not be complete without a chapter on words that have been literally and literarily born at the tip of a pen, for our language bestows a special kind of life upon people and places that have existed only in books. Fictional creations though they may be, many of these literary creations have assumed a vitality and longevity that pulse just as powerfully as their flesh-and-blood counterparts. The words that derive from these imaginary names can achieve such wide application that they are no longer written with capital letters.

Using the following descriptions, identify the common words that have sprung from the fertile imaginations of our novelists, playwrights, and poets. Also identify the original names:

1. The hero of a novel by Miguel Cervantes engaged himself in endless knightly quests, rescuing damsels he deemed to be in distress and fighting monsters by tilting against windmills. An adjective formed from his name now describes people who are idealistic and chivalrous to an extravagant degree.

2. The name of a blustering giant in Edmund Spenser's epic, *The Faerie Queene,* has become a word for a loudmouthed boaster who is notably short on performance.

3. Another big-talking giant lumbers through the pages of a novel by François Rabelais. This giant king was so huge that it took 17,913 cows to provide him with milk and 1,100 hides to make him a pair of shoes. Today an adjective form of his name denotes anything on a colossal scale.

4. In 1516 Sir Thomas More wrote a book about an ideal state. As a name for both the novel and the place, More coined a name from the Greek word parts *ou,* "no," *topos,* "place," and *-ia,* "state of being." The resulting word has come to designate any ideal society.

5. The imagination of Charles Dickens teemed with colorful characters who so embodied particular traits in human nature that their names have come to stand for those qualities. Thus, a fawning toadie is often called a *Uriah Heep* and a tyrannical teacher a *Gradgrind. Micawberish* has become a synonym for "habitually hopeful" and *Pecksniffery* a noun for religious hypocrisy. These name words have retained their capital letters, but one that is rapidly evolving into lowercase began life as a character in *A Christmas Carol.* Even though old Ebenezer's heart turned from stone to gold at the end of the story, we still use his name to describe a mean and miserly person.

A special kind of populist literature is the comic strip, and the cartoon characters and stories we encounter in our newspapers and on our movie screens have exerted a considerable influence on our language. The first successful American comic strip was "Yellow Kid" in Joseph Pulitzer's *New York World*. The feature made its debut in 1895 and was printed in attention-grabbing yellow ink. As early as 1898 the phrase *yellow journalism* was applied to sensational stories of crime and corruption that ran in papers like the *World*.

Identify the comic strip words that have not drawn their last breath as well as their pen-and-ink sources:

6. In 1928 Walt Disney gave the world a Mickey, an all-American rodent who performed heroic deeds and squeaked his undying love for Minnie. Soon after World War II world markets were flooded with wristwatches bearing this character's likeness. Because these watches were generally cheap affairs subject to chronic and chronometric mainspring breakdowns, people started associating anything shoddy or trivial with this character's name.

7. The name of H. T. Webster's wimpy comic strip character has become synonym for a meek, unassertive man.

8. Speaking of *wimpy*, linguists disagree about the origins of this vogue adjective. Some contend that *wimpy* is a form of the verb *whimper*. Others trace the word back to a potbellied fellow who devoured hamburgers in E. C. Segar's "Popeye" comic strip, which began in the late 1920s.

9. Another rotund comic strip character, this one created by David Low, inspired us to apply metaphorically the name of a floating airship to people endowed with an abundance of adipose tissue.

10. *On the* _____, meaning "not operating properly," may have started with one of the earliest comic strips, "The Katzenjammer Kids." Typically, the two hyperactive German boys caused all sorts of trouble for the Captain and other adults in the story.

Of all literary sources that feed into our English language, mythology is the richest. The world of classical mythology is essentially a human world. Realizing how splendid men and women could be, the Greeks and Romans made their gods and goddesses in their own images. And we who are alive today are so comfortable with these creations that we constantly speak and hear and write and read their names, even if we don't always know it.

Echo, for example, is an echo of a story that is more than two millennia old. Echo was a beautiful nymph who once upon a time aided Zeus in a love affair by keeping Hera, his wife, occupied in conversation. As a punishment for such verbal meddling, Hera confiscated Echo's power to initiate conversation and allowed her to repeat only the last words of anything she heard.

Such was a sorry-enough fate, but later Echo fell madly in love with an exceedingly handsome Greek boy, Narcissus, who, because of Echo's peculiar handicap, would have nothing to do with her. So deeply did the nymph grieve for her unrequited love that she wasted away to nothing until nothing was left but her voice, always repeating the last words she heard.

The fate that befell Narcissus explains why his name has been transformed into words like *narcissism* and *narcissistic,* pertaining to extreme self-love. One day Narcissus looked into a still forest lake and beheld his own face in the water, although he did not know it. He at once fell in love with the beautiful image just beneath the surface, and he, like Echo, pined away for a love that could never be consummated.

Identify the name-words that echo the names of the gods and goddesses, heroes and heroines, and fabulous creatures that inhabit the world of classical mythology as well as the eponymous progenitors of those words:

11. One of the vilest of mythology's villains was a king who served the body of his young son to the gods. They soon discovered the king's wicked ruse, restored the dead boy to life, and devised a punishment to fit the crime. They banished the king to Hades, where he is condemned to stand in a sparkling pool of water with boughs of luscious fruit overhead; when he stoops to drink, the water drains away through the bottom of the pool, and when he wishes to eat, the branches of fruit sway just out of his grasp. Ever since, when something presents itself temptingly to our view, we invoke this king's name.

12. An adjective that means "merry, inspiring mirth" comes from the name the ancient Romans gave to the king of their gods because it was a happy omen to be born under his influence.

13. The frenetic Greek nature god was said to cause sudden fear by darting out from behind bushes and frightening passersby. That fear now bears his name.

14. The gate to Hades, the Greek underworld, was guarded by a huge three-headed dog who fawned on those who entered but devoured those who sought to leave. It is easy to see why the name of this tri-headed creature has been transformed into an adjective that means "relating to the brain or intellect."

15. A Greek herald in Homer's *Iliad* was a human public-address system, for his voice could be heard all over camp. Today the adjective form of his name means "loud-voiced, bellowing."

16. The most famous of all Homer's creations spent ten years after the fall of Troy wandering through the ancient world encountering sorceresses and cyclopses (with 20/vision). The wily hero's name lives on in the word we use to describe a long journey or voyage marked by bizarre turns of events.

17. The hero Odysseus was tempted by creatures who were half woman, half bird who perched on rocks in the sea and lured ancient mariners to their deaths. Their piercing call has given us our word for the rising and falling whistle emitted by ambulances, fire engines, and police cars.

18. Another great Greek hero needed all his power to complete twelve exceedingly laborious labors. We use a form of his name to describe a mighty effort or an extraordinarily difficult task.

19. A tribe of female warriors cut off their right breasts in order to handle their bows more efficiently. The name of their tribe originally meant "breastless"; it now means a strong woman.

20. Because of its fluidity and mobility, quicksilver is identified by a more common label that is the Roman name for Hermes, the winged messenger of the gods. That name has also bequeathed us an adjective meaning "swift, eloquent, volatile."

(Answers on page 216)

NAME THAT BUNCH

(page 157)

1. mules **2.** clams **3.** ants **4.** rhinoceroses **5.** geese
6. leopards **7.** peacocks **8.** ducks **9.** owls **10.** locusts
11. lions **12.** fish **13.** foxes **14.** bears **15.** monkeys
16. ferrets **17.** hawks **18.** finches **19.** cats **20.** plovers
21. eagles **22.** quail **23.** woodpeckers **24.** squirrels
25. larks **26.** whales **27.** frogs **28.** crows **29.** starlings
30. storks **31.** pheasants **32.** doves **33.** wildfowl **34.** seals
35. turkeys **36.** martens **37.** wolves **38.** herons **39.** apes
40. boars **41.** swine **42.** magpies **43.** goats **44.** ravens
45. nightingales
46. eusuchian **47.** simian **48.** asinine **49.** ursine
50. apian **51.** avian **52.** taurine **53.** bovine **54.** cervine
55. diapsidian **56.** draconic **57.** aquiline **58.** elephantine
59. piscine **60.** vulpine **61.** ranine **62.** caprine **63.** equine
64. leonine **65.** musine **66.** porcine **67.** murine
68. batrachian **70.** lupine
71. nanny goat **72.** sow **73.** duck **74.** vixen **75.** goose
76. jenny **77.** peahen **78.** ewe **79.** dam **80.** mare
81. kit **82.** fledgling **83.** fawn **84.** elver **85.** fry
86. tadpole **87.** kid **88.** gosling **89.** cheeper **90.** leveret
91. eyas **92.** brit **93.** foal **94.** joey **95.** spat **96.** shoat
97. squab **98.** smolt **99.** cygnet **100.** poult

NAME THAT THINGAMABOB
(page 164)

1. ferrule   **2.** harp   **3.** plungers   **4.** pintle   **5.** aglet
6. chimb   **7.** bail   **8.** escutcheon   **9.** forel   **10.** tang
11. neb   **12.** keeper   **13.** ferrule   **14.** turnback   **15.** zarf
16. waist   **17.** paper bail   **18.** bobeche   **19.** bollard
20. muntins
21. frenulum   **22.** cerumen   **23.** opisthenar   **24.** vomer
25. philtrum   **26.** uvula   **27.** canthus   **28.** tragus   **29.** thenar
30. popliteal

FEAR OF PHOBIAS
(page 167)

1. apiophobia   **2.** taurophobia   **3.** aelurophobia
4. cynophobia   **5.** batarachophobia   **6.** hippophobia
7. musophobia   **8.** herpetophobia   **9.** galeophobia
10. arachnephobia
11. cometophobia   **12.** nyktophobia   **13.** elektrophobia
14. pyrophobia   **15.** thermophobia   **16.** photophobia
17. astraphobia   **18.** acousticophobia   **19.** heliophobia
20. aquaphobia
21. monophobia   **22.** automysophobia   **23.** ballistrophobia
24. hematophobia   **25.** logizomechanicophobia
26. demophobia   **27.** bathophobia   **28.** pharmacophobia
29. thanatophobia   **30.** claustrophobia
31. sociophobia   **32.** crystallophobia   **33.** bogyphobia
34. gerasophobia   **35.** cardiophobia   **36.** acrophobia
37. stygiophobia   **38.** gamophobia   **39.** triskaidecaphobia
40. agoraphobia
41. algophobia   **42.** cremnophobia   **43.** erotophobia
44. olfactophobia   **45.** tacophobia   **46.** glossophobia
47. chronophobia   **48.** emetophobia   **49.** verbaphobia
50. scriptophobia

AN ANTHOLOGY OF OLOGIES

(page 170)

1. the past through its artifacts   **2.** human customs   **3.** the influence of planets on life   **4.** hearing   **5.** life   **6.** the heart **7.** evil spirits   **8.** skin   **9.** organisms and environments **10.** embryos   **11.** contagious diseases   **12.** human races **13.** precious stones   **14.** one's ancestors   **15.** the earth's crust **16.** handwriting   **17.** weather   **18.** the nervous system **19.** birds   **20.** prisons   **21.** drugs   **22.** mind, emotions, behavior   **23.** earthquakes   **24.** God   **25.** poisons

26. spiders   **27.** whales   **28.** pornography   **29.** cells **30.** knowledge   **31.** aging   **32.** reptiles   **33.** living tissue **34.** fish   **35.** human movement   **36.** the throat   **37.** word patterns   **38.** fungi   **39.** ants   **40.** wine   **41.** existence   **42.** bones **43.** the ear   **44.** fossils   **45.** ancient documents   **46.** rocks **47.** literature and words   **48.** activities of organisms   **49.** beards **50.** symbols

FICTIONARY

(page 173)

1. c   **2.** a   **3.** d   **4.** d   **5.** a   **6.** b   **7.** c   **8.** a   **9.** d **10.** c   **11.** b   **12.** d

WHAT'S IN A NAME?

(page 177)

1. Irving Berlin   **2.** William Holden   **3.** Angie Dickinson **4.** Helen Hayes   **5.** Charles Bronson   **6.** James Garner   **7.** Red Buttons   **8.** Kirk Douglas   **9.** Engelbert Humperdinck **10.** Elton John

11. Cyd Charisse   **12.** Dyan Cannon   **13.** Tab Hunter **14.** Greta Garbo   **15.** Judy Garland   **16.** Natalie Wood **17.** Soupy Sales   **18.** Loretta Young   **19.** Tiny Tim **20.** Simone Signoret

21. Hugh O'Brian   **22.** Jack Benny   **23.** Cher   **24.** Cary

Grant **25.** Michael Caine **26.** Stevie Wonder **27.** Lauren Bacall **28.** Mick Jagger **29.** Boris Karloff **30.** Tammy Wynette
31. Redd Foxx **32.** Rock Hudson **33.** Tony Curtis
34. Sophia Loren **35.** Roy Rogers **36.** Ringo Starr **37.** Raquel Welch **38.** Judy Holliday **39.** Bob Dylan **40.** Sandra Dee

THE GAME IS THE NAME

(page 181)

1. bailiff **2.** baker **3.** beer manufacturer **4.** candlemaker
5. clerk **6.** priest **7.** coal miner **8.** barrel maker **9.** potter
10. falconer
11. arrow maker **12.** keeper of fences **13.** bargeman
14. keeper of the cupboard **15.** leather worker **16.** bricklayer
17. doorkeeper **18.** carpenter **19.** shoemaker **20.** scholar
21. sty warden **22.** roofer **23.** toll-bridge collector
24. wheel maker **25.** weaver

AUTHOR! AUTHOR! AUTHOR!

(page 185)

1. Edgar Poe **2.** Ben Williams **3.** Katherine Porter
4. Edwin Robinson **5.** Thomas Macaulay **6.** Thomas Aldrich
7. Elizabeth Browning **8.** Harriet Stowe **9.** George Shaw
10. Clare Luce
11. James Cabell **12.** Richard Sheridan **13.** Charles Brown
14. William Yeats **15.** Percy Shelley **16.** William Williams
17. Joel Harris **18.** Clement Moore **19.** Arthur Doyle
20. John Ransome
21. William Bryant **22.** Henry Thoreau **23.** William Howells 24. James Cooper **25.** Dante Rossetti **26.** John Whittier
27. Laura Wilder **28.** George Nathan **29.** Marjorie Rawlings
30. Paul Dunbar
31. Ernest Thayer **32.** Edgar Masters **33.** Robert Stevenson **34.** William Thackery **35.** Gerard Hopkins **36.** Louisa Alcott **37.** John Synge **38.** Zora Hurston **39.** Sarah Jewett
40. Albert Terhune
41. Robert Warren **42.** Finley Dunne **43.** Edgar Bur-

roughs **44.** James Lowell **45.** Edna Millay **46.** William Landor **47.** Erle Gardner **48.** Stephen Benet **49.** Henry Longfellow **50.** Ralph Emerson

51. Julia Howe or Henry Beecher **52.** James Johnson **53.** Oliver Holmes **54.** James Riley **55.** Arthur Pinero

56. Milne **57.** Housman **58.** Cronin **59.** Snow **60.** Lewis **61.** Lawrence **62.** Thomas **63.** White **64.** Cummings **65.** Doctorow **66.** Forster **67.** Scott Fitzgerald **68.** Wells **69.** Munro **70.** Mencken

71. Lovecraft **72.** Priestley **73.** Salinger **74.** Ballard **75.** Donleavy **76.** Tolkien **77.** Frank Baum **78.** Henry **79.** James **80.** Wodehouse

81. Laing **82.** Hinton **83.** Perelman **84.** Pearson **85.** Eliot **86.** Andrews **87.** Pritchett **88.** Somerset Maugham **89.** DuBois **90.** Auden

91. Stendhal **92.** George Orwell **93.** Mark Twain **94.** Lewis Carroll **95.** George Eliot **96.** Dr. Seuss **97.** Joseph Conrad **98.** Saki **99.** O. Henry **100.** James Herriot

IMMORTAL MORTALS

(page 191)

1. sandwich-Sandwich **2.** maverick-Maverick **3.** geronimo!-Geronimo **4.** bloomers-Bloomer **5.** boycott-Boycott **6.** mesmerize-Mesmer **7.** spoonerism-Spooner **8.** chauvinism-Chauvin **9.** sideburns-Burnside **10.** melba toast, peach melba-Melba

11. pompadour-Pompadour **12.** ritzy, the ritz-Ritz **13.** leotards-Léotard **14.** poinsettia-Ponsett **15.** gerrymander-Gerry **16.** macadam, macadamize-McAdam **17.** dunce-Duns **18.** bowdlerize-Bowdler **19.** galvanize-Galvani **20.** graham cracker-Graham

A JIM-DANDY QUIZ

(page 197)

1. jackrabbit **2.** jackass **3.** jackdaw **4.** jackal **5.** jack-in-the-pulpit **6.** jackknife **7.** jack-in-the-box **8.** jack-of-all-trades **9.** jackpot **10.** jackhammer

11. blackjack   **12.** flapjacks   **13.** lumberjack
14. jackstraws **15.** hijack **16.** jack **17.** jacket **18.** jackanape
19. jackboot **20.** crackerjack

21. bobsled **22.** bobby socks **23.** bobby pin **24.** bobbed
hair **25.** bobcat **26.** bobolink **27.** bobwhite **28.** bobtail
29. bobbin

30. tomcat **31.** tommy gun **32.** tomahawk **33.** tomboy
34. tomfoolery **35.** tommyrot **36.** tom-tom

37. longjohns **38.** johnny-jump-up **39.** johnnycake
40. the john

41. billy club **42.** billygoat **43.** hillbilly **44.** billiards
45. billow **46.** a billion

47. jimmies **48.** jimmy **49.** jimjams **50.** jim-dandy

PUTTING WORDS IN THEIR PLACES

(page 200)

1. bikini-Bikini **2.** limerick-Limerick **3.** blarney-Blarney
4. marathon-Marathon **5.** to shanghai-Shanghai **6.** bedlam-
Bethlehem **7.** donnybrook-Donnybrook **8.** tuxedo-Tuxedo
Park **9.** turkey-Turkey **10.** laconic-Laconia

ENGLISH THROWS THE BOOK AT US

(page 205)

1. quixotic-Don Quixote **2.** braggadocio-Braggadocio
3. gargantuan-Gargantua **4.** utopia-*Utopia* **5.** scrooge-Scrooge

6. mickey mouse-Mickey Mouse **7.** milquetoast-Caspar
Milquetoast **8.** J. Wellington Wimpy **9.** blimp-Colonel Blimp
10. fritz-Fritz

11. tantalize-Tantalus **12.** jovial-Jove **13.** panic-Pan
14. cerebral-Cerberus **15.** stentorian-Stentor **16.** odyssey-
Odysseus **17.** siren-the sirens **18.** herculean-Hercules
19. amazon-Amazons **20.** mercury, mercurial-Mercury

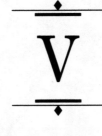

V

DICTION

"Fine words butter no parsnips."
—ENGLISH PROVERB

◆ POMPOUS PROVERBS

When we speak and write, we generally try to say something. We call upon our vocabulary to select those words and expressions that will best communicate to others what we have in mind. This process of choosing words to express ideas and emotions is called diction. We move up and down levels of diction when we decide how formal or informal, how abstract or concrete, how common or uncommon, and how big or small will be the words in which we cast our messages.

When I was a callow youth, my neighborhood buddies and I used to sing a learned lyric that played around with levels of diction:

> *Perambulate, perambulate, perambulate your craft*
> *Placidly down the liquid solution.*
> *Ecstatically, ecstatically, ecstatically, ecstatically,*
> *Existence is but a delusion.*

Translated into clear and simple English, our polysyllabic poem turned out to be *Row, row, row your boat . . .*

These days my youthful adventure in oblique obfuscation and polysyllabic poetry has evolved into a challenging game of circumlocutory clichés. The popularity of this game may be founded on our fascination with big words— or on the fact that so many people actually write that way!

What follows is a list of simple, everyday adages, bromides, quotations, proverbs, saws, and general folk wisdom that have been written in inflated, jargonized English. Your task is to translate each sesquipedalian statement back into its original, nonorchidaceous form. For example, "Under no circumstances should you compute the quantity of your barnyard fowl previous to their incubation" emerges as "Don't count your chickens before they're hatched."

For starters, match the five reclassified classics with the five everyday classics that follow:

1. Eschew the implement of correction and vitiate the scion.

2. The policy of being sapient is injudicious where the opposite condition confers felicity.

3. Surveillance should precede saltation.

4. A timorous cardiovascular pump at no time succeeds in acquiring the pulchritudinous distaff.

5. Gramineous organisms are perpetually more verdant when located on an adjacent surface.

　a. The grass is always greener on the other side.
　b. Spare the rod and spoil the child.
　c. Look before you leap.
　d. Faint heart never won fair maiden.
　e. Where ignorance is bliss, 'tis folly to be wise.

The answers are 1.b, 2.e, 3.c, 4.d, and 5.a.

What I hope you'll discover from all this puffery is that those of superior intelligence quotient require not effusive verbosity. In other, simpler words, a word to the wise is sufficient. Take your time and remember that precipitancy generates prodigality. That is, haste makes waste.

1. The stylus is more potent than the claymore.

2. Pulchritude possesses exclusively cutaneous profundity.

3. It is futile to attempt to indoctrinate a superannuated canine with innovative maneuvers.

4. The greatest of need is the maternal parent of the art of original contrivance.

5. A revolving lithic conglomerate accrues no lichen.

6. Everything is legitimate in matters pertaining to ardent affections and international armed conflicts.

7. The temperature of the aqueous content of a metallic receptacle under unremitting surveillance does not attain its level of evaporation.

8. Members of an avian species of identical plumage congregate.

9. Freedom from incrustations of grime is contiguous to rectitude.

10. It is fruitless to endure lacrimation over precipitately departed lacteal fluid.

11. Similar sire, similar scion.

12. Pulchritude reposes within the optic parameters of the perceiver.

13. Sorting on the part of mendicants must be interdicted.

14. Where there are visible emissions from carbonaceous materials, there exists conflagration.

15. Male cadavers are incapable of yielding any testimony.

16. Integrity is the superlative strategy.

17. A plethora of individuals with expertise in culinary techniques vitiates the potable concoction.

18. Eleemosynary deeds have their incipience domestically.

19. All articles that coruscate with resplendence are not, ipso facto, auriferous.

20. An addlepated individual and his specie divaricate with prematurity.

21. The ultimate entity of dried gramineous organism induces a rupture of the dorsal portion of the ship of the desert.

22. Hubris antedates a gravity-impelled descent.

23. Three quarters of a dozen individual movements

by a slender sewing instrument may be obviated by the utilization of a single, opportunistic thrust of said instrument.

24. Exclusive dedication to necessitous employment without interludes of hedonistic diversion renders John a hebtudinous young person.

25. Soft airs possess the potency to mitigate the anguish residual in the barbaric thorax.

26. Minuscule erudition jeopardizes security.

27. Consolidated we maintain ourselves erect; bifurcated we plummet.

28. A feathered biped in the terminal part of the arm equals the value of a brace of such creatures in densely branched shrubbery.

29. Persons deficient in judgment hasten to undertake that for which winged celestials hesitate to assume responsibility.

30. Individuals who make their abode in vitreous edifices of patent frangibility are advised to refrain from catapulting petrous projectiles.

31. A recently purchased implement for removing floor grime invariably eliminates such grime most efficiently.

32. A single graphic facsimile is appraised in excess of myriad articulations.

33. Measurable duration and the alternate rise and fall of oceanic substance under lunar influence tarry not for Homo sapiens.

34. A precipitate avian ensnares the vermiculate creature.

35. The person emitting the ultimate cachinnation possesses thereby the optimal cachinnation.

36. Sugary condiments secure initial pleasure, but fermented grain is decidedly more parsimonious of time.

37. Trust should never be extended to Hellenic inhabitants transporting items for gratuitous dispersal.

38. Rectitude does not attach itself to binary transgressions.

39. Each canine possesses its period of preeminence.

40. Precocious entry into a somnolent condition succeeded by precocious reentry into a scheduled plan of activities will maximize salubrious conditions, remunerative gains, and sapience.

41. The depth of nocturnal gloom becomes most stygian just prior to the appearance of eastern solar photons.

42. Missiles of ligneous or osterous consistency have the potential of fracturing my osseous structure, but vocalized appellations eternally remain benocuous.

43. Refrain from enumerating the denta of gratuitous members of the Equidae family.

44. Fondness for lucre constitutes the tuberous structure of all satanically inspired principles.

45. You cannot estimate the value of a bound narrative from its exterior vesture.

46. A single Pyrus Malus per diem restrains the arrival of the Hippocratic apostle.

47. Adorn yourself with the comfortable pedal encasement.

48. Cleave gramineous matter for fodder during the period when the orb of day is refulgent.

49. Aberration is the hallmark of Homo sapiens, while longanimous placability and condonation are the indicia of supermundane omniscience.

50. Although it is within the realm of possibility to escort equus caballus to a location providing a potable mixture of hydrogen and oxygen, one cannot coerce said mammal to imbibe.

(Answers on page 235)

◆ STAMP OUT DOUBLESPEAK!*

In recent years we have come to realize that our air and water and land are threatened by pollution. Less observable is the fouling of another natural resource, our English language. A stream can tolerate and absorb a certain amount of waste. Beyond a given volume, garbage creates a life-threatening imbalance. So it is with words. When enough messages enter the environment that say what is not believed and use language to varnish the truth, our words become polluted. James Lipton has written, "Our language, one of our most precious natural resources, is also a dwindling one that deserves at least as much protection as our woodlands, streams, and whooping cranes." As we grow in awareness of how precious and fragile our world is, we can make our earth, our air, our water—and our language—purer, more beautiful environments in which life can survive and flourish.

One group that strives to protect and purify our language is the Committee on Public Doublespeak, an arm of the National Council of Teachers of English. Doublespeak doesn't call a spade a spade. Rather doublespeak calls a spade a heart, or a "manual excavation device." Established in 1973, the Doublespeak Committee aims to stanch the spew of dishonest, misleading, and inhumane language, especially regarding public policy.

Below are sixty examples of grossly euphemistic language that the Committee on Public Doublespeak has

---

* This game is adapted from material published by the NCTE Committee on Public Doublespeak and is used with permission.

doublespeaker

captured through news media reports. These are all real examples; they are not made up. In each cluster, translate the doublespeak into good, clear singlespeak—plain English, that is—by matching items in the two columns. In some instances one translation applies to several entries of doublespeak:

What's My Line?	*Translation*
1. automotive internist	dry cleaner
2. urban transportation specialist	repairman
	dishwasher
3. nail technician	junk dealer
4. media courier	manicurist
5. sex industry worker	window washer
6. interment excavation expert	elevator operator
	cab or bus driver
7. entropy control engineer	prostitute
8. transparent wall engineer	janitor
9. utensil maintainer	checkout clerk
10. animal control warden	dog catcher
11. clothing refresher	car mechanic
12. service technician	newspaper deliverer
13. member of vertical transportation corps	grave digger
14. auto dismantler and recycler	
15. career associate scanning professional	

Sociology Doublespeak	*Translation*
16. disadvantaged	riot
17. non–goal-oriented member of society	poor
	death house
18. correctional facility	slum, ghetto

19. fiscal underachievers   bum, street person
20. capital sentences unit   prison
21. civil disorder
22. economically nonaffluent
23. inner city

Commercial Doublespeak   *Translation*

24. previously owned   for our convenience
25. genuine imitation   false teeth
26. interdental stimulator   girdle
27. occasional irregularity   toilet paper
28. facial quality tissue   toothpick
29. form persuader   sliced
30. dentures   constipation
31. experienced   fake
32. portion controlled   greeting cards
33. social expression products   used
34. for your convenience

Employment Doublespeak   *Translation*

35. reclassified   fired
36. outplaced
37. nonretained
38. deselected
39. nonpositively terminated
40. downsizing of personnel

Military Doublespeak   *Translation*

41. nuclear device   retreat
42. enhanced radiation device   civilian deaths
43. incursion   overthrow
44. pre-dawn vertical insertion   nuclear bomb
45. protective reaction strike   peace

Military Doublespeak	Translation
46. permanent prehostility	invasion
47. governmental unconsoli-dation	invasion with parachutes
48. redeployment	bombing
49. backloading	
50. collateral casualties	

Death Doublespeak	Translation
51. negative patient-care out-come	malpractice
52. therapeutic misadventure	cemetery
53. memorial park	death
54. deprivation of life	dying
55. death situation	killing

Economic Doublespeak	Translation
56. revenue enhancement	tax
57. user's fee	tax increase
58. tax reform	stock market crash
59. negative investment increment	loss
60. equity retreat	

Before you check your answers, remember that as the Doublespeak Committee has pointed out, "Nothing in life is certain except negative patient-care outcome and revenue enhancement."

(Answers on page 236)

◆ ## HIGHLY IRREGULAR VERBS

Most words have two kinds of meaning. The basic, direct meaning we call denotation. The implied, suggestive meanings—connotations—are what give a word its individuality and color, its distinctive and unique personality.

Take the word *fist*, defined denotatively as "the hand clenched with the fingers pressed into the palm and the thumb pressed around the fingers." Then "the maiden held the white lily in her delicate fist" ought to be a perfectly correct sentence. We smile, however, at the clashing connotations of *maiden, lily,* and *delicate* on the one hand and *fist* on the other, and clenched, hand. The denotation of *fist* is correct, but its connotations make it a grotesque choice for the sentence about the maiden and the lily.

Giggle has been defined as "to laugh with repeated short catches of breath." But because of its connotations, *giggled* is strikingly misplaced in a sentence like "the grizzled cowhand giggled at the tenderfoot's foolish suggestions."

The British philosopher and mathematician Bertrand Russell enjoyed fooling around with the connotations of words. On a British Broadcasting Company radio program called *The Brain Trust,* Russell presented the following "conjugation" of an "irregular verb":

I am firm.
You are obstinate.
He is a pig-headed fool.

a pig-headed fool

As the "Grammar Grappler" for _Writer's Digest,_ a monthly magazine for writers, I recently ran a contest inviting readers to submit their best irregular verbs based on Russell's irreverent model and following these rules:

- Each conjugation must proceed from _I_ through _you_ to _he_ or _she._
- The basic denotation of the concept in each cluster must be maintained.
- In each triad the connotations must grow increasingly mean-spirited as the conjugation moves from first to second to third person (_he_ or _she_).
- Humor and verbal sparkle earn extra points.

I was inundated with more than two thousand entries, plunging me into a state of conjugational bliss. Here are some of the best submissions as they appeared in the October 1989 issue of _Writer's Digest:_

- I am a concerned parent. You tend to interfere. She writes in her daughter's diary.
- I am beautiful. You are pretty. She has a good personality.
- I have a dream. You are a dreamer. He lives in a dreamworld.
- I can eat off the floor. You do your best to be clean. She can eat off the floor because her floor is covered with food.
- I am affectionate. You are libidinous. She has hinges on her heels.

As a demonstration of your denotation-connotation imagination, try creating your own concatenations of irregular verbs.

♦ VERBS WITH VERVE

Researchers showed groups of test subjects a picture of an automobile accident and then asked this question: "How fast were the cars going when they __ ?" The blank was variously filled in with *bumped, contacted, hit, collided,* or *smashed.* Groups that were asked "How fast were the cars going when they smashed?" responded with the highest estimates of speed.

All of which proves that verbs create specific images in the mind's eye. Because verbs are the words in a sentence that express action and movement, they are the spark plugs of effective style. The more specific the verbs you choose in your speaking and writing, the more sparky will be the images you flash on the minds of your listeners and readers.

Suppose you write, " 'No,' she said and left the room." Grammatically there is nothing wrong with this sentence. But because the verbs *say* and *leave* are among the most general and colorless in the English language, you have missed the chance to create a vivid word picture. Consider the alternatives:

———————— ◆ ————————

SAID

———————— ◆ ————————

apologized	jabbered
asserted	minced
blubbered	mumbled
blurted	murmured
boasted	shrieked
cackled	sighed
commanded	slurred
drawled	snapped
giggled	sobbed
groaned	whispered
gurgled	whooped

———————— ◆ ————————

LEFT

———————— ◆ ————————

backed	sauntered
bolted	skipped
bounced	staggered
crawled	stamped
darted	stole
flew	strode
hobbled	strutted
lurched	stumbled
marched	tiptoed
plodded	wandered
pranced	whirled

If you had chosen from among these vivid verbs and had crafted the sentence " 'No,' she sobbed, and stumbled out of the room," you would have created a powerful picture of something quite distraught.

Here are brief descriptions of twenty different people. Choosing from the two lists of synonyms for *said* and *left*, fill in the blanks of the sentence " 'No,' he/she _____, and _____ the room." Select the pair of verbs that best create the most vivid picture of each person described. Throughout your answers try to use as many different verbs as you can:

1. an angry person
2. a baby
3. a braggart
4. a child
5. a clown
6. a confused person
7. a cowboy/cowgirl
8. someone crying
9. a drunkard
10. an embarrassed person
11. an excited person
12. a frightened person
13. a happy person
14. someone in a hurry
15. an injured person
16. a military officer
17. a sneaky person
18. a timid person
19. a tired person
20. a witch

(Answers on page 237)

♦ ANSWERS

POMPOUS PROVERBS

(page 219)

1. The pen is mightier than the sword. **2.** Beauty is only skin deep. **3.** You can't teach an old dog new tricks. **4.** Necessity is the mother of invention. **5.** A rolling stone gathers no moss. **6.** All's fair in love and war. **7.** A watched pot never boils. **8.** Birds of a feather flock together. **9.** Cleanliness is next to godliness. **10.** Don't cry over spilled milk.

11. Like father, like son. **12.** Beauty is in the eye of the beholder. **13.** Beggars can't be choosers. **14.** Where there's smoke, there's fire. **15.** Dead men tell no tales. **16.** Honesty is the best policy. **17.** Too many cooks spoil the broth. **18.** Charity begins at home. **19.** All that glitters is not gold. **20.** A fool and his money are soon parted.

21. The straw that broke the camel's back. **22.** Pride goes before a fall. **23.** A stitch in time saves nine. **24.** All work and no play makes Jack a dull boy. **25.** Music has charms to soothe a savage breast. **26.** A little learning is a dangerous thing. **27.** United we stand; divided we fall. **28.** A bird in the hand is worth two in the bush. **29.** Fools rush in where angels fear to tread. **30.** People who live in glass houses shouldn't throw stones.

31. A new broom sweeps clean. **32.** A picture is worth a thousand words. **33.** Time and tide wait for no man. **34.** The early bird catches the worm. **35.** He who laughs last laughs best. **36.** Candy is dandy, but liquor is quicker. **37.** Beware of Greeks bearing gifts. **38.** Two wrongs don't make a right. **39.** Every dog has its day. **40.** Early to bed and early to rise makes a man healthy, wealthy, and wise.

41. It's always darkest just before the light. **42.** Sticks and stones may break my bones, but names will never hurt me. **43.** Don't look a gift horse in the mouth. **44.** The love of money is the root of all evil. **45.** You can't judge a book by its cover. **46.** An apple a day keeps the doctor away. **47.** If the shoe fits, wear it. **48.** Make hay while the sun shines. **49.** To err is human, to forgive divine. **50.** You can lead a horse to water, but you can't make it drink.

STAMP OUT DOUBLESPEAK!

(page 224)

1. car mechanic   **2.** cab or bus driver   **3.** manicurist **4.** newspaper delivery person   **5.** prostitute   **6.** grave digger **7.** janitor   **8.** window washer   **9.** dishwasher   **10.** dog catcher **11.** dry cleaner   **12.** repairman   **13.** elevator operator   **14.** junk dealer   **15.** checkout clerk

16. poor   **17.** bum, street person   **18.** prison   **19.** poor **20.** death house   **21.** riot   **22.** poor   **23.** slum, ghetto

24. used   **25.** fake   **26.** toothpick   **27.** constipation **28.** tiolet paper   **29.** girdle   **30.** false teeth   **31.** used **32.** sliced   **33.** greeting cards   **34.** for our convenience

35. fired   **36.** fired   **37.** fired   **38.** fired   **39.** fired **40.** fired

41. nuclear bomb   **42.** nuclear bomb   **43.** invasion **44.** invasion with parachutes   **45.** invasion   **46.** peace **47.** overthrow   **48.** retreat   **49.** retreat   **50.** civilian deaths

51. death   **52.** malpractice   **53.** cemetery   **54.** killing **55.** death

56. tax increase   **57.** tax   **58.** tax increase   **59.** loss **60.** stock market crash

VERBS WITH VERVE

(page 232)
(OTHER PAIRINGS ARE POSSIBLE)

1. snapped—stamped   2. gurgled—crawled   3. boasted—strutted   4. minced or giggled—skipped, bounced, or pranced   5. giggled—bounced or skipped   6. mumbled—stumbled   7. drawled—sauntered   8. blubbered or sobbed—staggered, lurched, or stumbled   9. slurred—lurched or staggered   10. apologized—bolted

11. jabbered or blurted—whirled   12. shrieked—dashed or bolted   13. whooped—pranced   14. blurted—dashed or bolted   15. moaned—hobbled   16. commanded—marched or strode   17. whispered—stole   18. murmured—tiptoed or stole   19. sighed—plodded   20. cackled—flew

VI

LOGIC

"Most people would die sooner than think;
in fact, they do so."

—BERTRAND RUSSELL

◆ GOTCHA!

Read the following nursery rhyme and then answer the question posed in the last line:

> *As I was going to St. Ives,*
> *I met a man with seven wives.*
> *Every wife had seven sacks.*
> *Every sack had seven cats.*
> *Every cat had seven kits.*
> *Kits, cats, sacks, wives—*
> *How many were going to St. Ives?*

The answer to the question is one. While the man and his wives and their sacks, cats, and kits were going *from* St. Ives, only the speaker—the "I" in the rhyme—was going *to* St. Ives.

If you madly multiplied 7 times 7 times 7 times 7 and added one for the man, you were the victim of a language trap. Language traps are brief posers that test your ability to read or listen carefully and to avoid being fooled by misleading information. If you think precisely as you consider the thirty-five classic language traps in this chapter, you can avoid being caught by the snapping shut of steel jaws.

1. Which is correct: "Nine and seven is fifteen" or "Nine and seven are fifteen"?

2. How many three-cent stamps are there in a dozen?

3. Pronounce out loud the words formed by each of the following letter series: B-O-A-S-T, C-O-A-S-T, R-O-A-S-T. Now, what do you put in a toaster?

4. A doctor is about to operate on a little boy. "This child is my son!" exclaims the doctor. The doctor is correct, yet the doctor is not the boy's father. What is going on?

5. If a peacock and a half lays an egg and a half in a day and a half, how many eggs will three peacocks lay in three days?

6. Do they have a Fourth of July in England?

7. Two men play five games of checkers, and each wins the same number of games. There are no draws. How can this be?

8. A farmer had seventeen sheep. All but nine died. How many were left alive?

9. If a bus leaves from Boston for New York City an hour before another bus leaves from New York City for Boston, which bus will be closer to Boston when the two are passing each other?

10. A rope ladder is hanging over the side of a ship. The ladder is twelve feet long, and the rungs are one foot apart, with the lowest rung resting on the surface of the water. How long will it take before the first three rungs are underwater.

11. What was the highest mountain on earth before Mount Everest was discovered?

12. What were Alexander Graham Bell's first words?

13. If two is company and three is a crowd, what are four and five?

14. How many times can you subtract 5 from 25?

15. How much dirt is there in a hole three feet by three feet by three feet?

16. In the United States is it legal for a man to marry his widow's sister?

17. Pronounce out loud the word formed by each of the following letter series: M-A-C-D-O-N-A-L-D, M-A-C-B-E-T-H, M-A-C-H-I-N-E-R-Y.

18. One child playing on a beach has made four and

a half sand piles. Another child has made two and a half sand piles. They decide to put all their sand piles together. How many sand piles do they now have?

19. A dog is tied to a twenty-foot leash yet is able to run to a bone lying fifty feet away. The leash does not stretch or break in any way. How is this possible?

20. I have in my hand two U.S. coins that total thirty cents. One is not a nickel. What are the two coins?

21. How many mistakes can you find in this sentence? "Their are five mistaiks in this sentence."

22. Read the following sentence slowly and only once, counting the number of *F*'s:

FINISHED FILES ARE THE RESULT
OF YEARS OF SCIENTIFIC STUDY

How many *F*'s did you find?

23. If an airplane crashes on the Maine–New Hampshire border, in which state would the survivors be buried?

24. Mary and Jane were born on the same day of the same year of the same father and mother. They look almost exactly alike, yet they are not twins. How can this be?

25. Which is correct: "The capitol of Pennsylvania is Philadelphia" or "The capital of Pennsylvania is Philadelphia"?

26. If you drop a rock, would it fall more rapidly through water at 40 degrees Fahrenheit or 20 degrees Fahrenheit?

27. Attempting to get out of a well that is thirty feet deep, a frog, starting at the bottom, hops up three feet and falls back two with each attempt. How many tries will it take the frog to reach the top of the well?

28. I have five sisters, and each of my sisters has a brother. How many children did my parents have?

29. The number of people in a movie theater doubles every five minutes. After an hour, the theater is full. When was the theater half full?

30. You are the engineer on a train going from Chicago to New York. The train leaves Chicago with a hundred passengers, stops in Detroit to pick up ten and discharge five, stops in Cleveland to pick up five and discharge ten, stops in Buffalo to pick up ten and discharge five, and then proceeds to New York.

How old is the engineer?

(Answers on page 267)

◆ FIGURING OUT AUNT MATILDA

My aunt Matilda is a very peculiar relative, a woman of strong likes and dislikes. For example, Aunt Matilda likes apples but not oranges and tennis but not golf. She likes supper but not lunch and butter but not margarine. She likes waffles but not pancakes and jazz but not rock.

It took me a long time to realize that Aunt Matilda likes words that contain double consonants. In fact, all of my aunt Matilda's steadfast opinions can be explained by the patterns of letters or sounds in words. You can test your sense of logic by trying to figure out my aunt Matilda's likes and dislikes. Examine each list and state the reason for Aunt Matilda's preferences:

1. Aunt Matilda likes aarvarks but not anteaters.
   She likes bees but not wasps.
   She likes boots but not shoes.
   She likes vacuum cleaners but not mops.
   She likes beets but not turnips.
   She likes rooms but not closets.
2. Aunt Matilda likes sports but not athaletics.
   She likes restaurants but not pizzarias.
   She likes seniors but not sophmores.
   She likes commerce but not bussiness.
   She likes usage but not grammer.
   She likes floors but not cielings.
3. Aunt Matilda likes birthdays but not anniversaries.
   She likes cupcakes but not pastries.

She likes suitcases but not luggage.
She likes highways but not roads.
She likes baseball but not hockey.
She likes airplanes but not trains.

4. Aunt Matilda likes oboes but not clarinets.
She likes picnics but not outings.
She likes downtown but not uptown.
She likes voodoo but not magic.
She likes redheads but not brunettes.
She likes singing but not dancing.

5. Aunt Matilda likes Mom but not Grandmother.
She likes Dad but not Grandfather.
She likes a Toyota but not a Honda.
She likes noon but not night.
She likes radar but not television.

6. Aunt Matilda likes pets but not dogs.
She likes golf but not squash.
She likes pool but not billiards.
She likes rats but not mice.
She likes flow but not ebb.
She likes desserts but not snacks.

7. Aunt Matilda likes seas but not oceans.
She likes pains but not aches.
She likes carrots but not potatoes.
She likes maize but not corn.
She likes lye but not bleach.
She likes beets but not turnips.

8. Aunt Matilda likes detergent but not bleach.
She likes mascara but not makeup.
She likes lipstick but not rouge.
She likes condors but not falcons.
She likes murmurs but not whispers.
She likes Tennessee but not Georgia.

9. Aunt Matilda likes algebra but not geometry.
She likes stones but not rocks.

She likes gabbing but not gossip.
She likes trout but not salmon.
She likes health but not illness.
She likes pomp but not circumstance.

10. Aunt Matilda likes chestnuts but not walnuts.
    She likes armies but not navies.
    She likes legends but not myths.
    She likes hippies but not protestors.
    She likes chinchilla but not mink.
    She likes ribbon but not trim.

11. Aunt Matilda likes nobody but not somebody.
    She likes staples but not tacks.
    She likes bugles but not trumpets.
    She likes demons but not devils.
    She likes signs but not billboards.
    She likes posters but not impostors.

12. Aunt Matilda likes pears but not peaches.
    She likes talks but not speeches.
    She likes campers but not hikers.
    She likes tables but not chairs.
    She likes mothers but not fathers.
    She likes platters but not dishes.

(Answers on page 268)

♦ DIG DOWN TO THE ROOTS*

Words and people have a lot in common. Like people, words are born, grow up, get married, have children, and even die. And, like people, words come in families—big and beautiful families. A word family is a cluster of words that are related because they contain the same root; a root is a basic building block of language from which a variety of related words are formed. You can expand your vocabulary by digging down to the roots of an unfamiliar word and identifying the meanings of those roots.

For example, knowing that the roots *scribe* and *script* mean "write" will help you to deduce the meanings of a prolific clan of words, including *ascribe, conscript, describe, inscribe, manuscript, nondescript, postscript, prescribe, proscribe, scribble, scripture,* and *transcribe.* For another example, once you know that *dic* and *dict* are roots that mean "speak or say," you possess a key that unlocks the meanings of tens of related words, including *abdicate, benediction, contradict, dedicate, dictator, dictaphone, dictionary, dictum, edict, indicate, indict, interdict, malediction, predict, syndicate, valedictory, verdict, vindicate,* and *vindictive.*

Suppose that you encounter the word *antipathy* in speech or writing. From words like *antiwar* and *antifreeze* you can infer that the root *anti* means "against," and from words like *sympathy* and *apathy* that *path* is a root that means "feeling." From such insights it is but a short leap to deduce that *antipathy* means "feeling against some-

---

*This game is adapted from Richard Lederer and Deborah Boettiger, *SAT Vocabulary Flash Cards* (Amsco)

thing." This process of rooting out illustrates the old saying "It's hard by the yard but a cinch by the inch."

Now let's cultivate an acre of roots, fifty word parts descended from either Latin or Greek, each followed by three words containing each root. From the meanings of the clue words, deduce the meaning of each root, as in PHON—microphone, phonics, telephone = *sound*. Good luck. I'm rooting for you!

1. ARCH—archangel, archbishop, monarch = _____
2. ANTHROP—anthropology, misanthrope, philanthropy = _____
3. AUTO—autobiography, autograph, automaton = _____
4. BIO—biodegradable, biology, biosphere = _____
5. CAPET—capital, decapitate, per capita = _____
6. CHRON—chronic, chronology, synchronize = _____
7. CRAT—aristocrat, autocrat, democratic = _____
8. CRED—credit, creed, incredible = _____
9. CULP—culpable, culprit, exculpate = _____
10. EU—eugenics, eulogy, euphemism = _____
11. FID—confide, fidelity, perfidy = _____
12. GEN—genetic, genre, homogeneous = _____
13. GRAPH—autograph, biography, graphology = _____
14. GRAV—aggravate, grave, gravitation = _____

15. GREG—congregation, gregarious,
    segregate = _____
16. HYDRO—dehydrated, hydrant,
    hydroelectric = _____
17. LEG—legal, legislate,
    legitimate = _____
18. LEV—alleviate, elevate,
    levity = _____
19. LOQU—eloquent, loquacious,
    soliloquy = _____
20. MAGN—magnanimous, magnify,
    magnitude = _____
21. MAL—malady, malediction,
    malevolent = _____
22. MISS—dismiss, missile,
    transmission = _____
23. NOV—innovation, novelty,
    renovate = _____
24. OMNI—omnipotent, omniscient,
    omnivorous = _____
25. ONYM—anonymous, pseudonym,
    synonym = _____
26. ORTH—orthodontist, orthodox,
    orthopedic = _____
27. PAN—panacea, pandemonium,
    panoramic = _____
28. PED—expedition, pedal,
    pedestrian = _____
29. PEL—compel, propel,
    repel = _____
30. PHIL—bibliophile, philanthropy,
    philology = _____
31. POLY—polygamy, polyglot,
    polygon = _____
32. PORT—export, portable,
    transportation = _____

33. PRIM—primal, primeval, primitive = _____

34. SENT—consent, resent, sentimental = _____

35. SEQU—consecutive, obsequious, sequential = _____

36. SIMIL—assimilate, similarity, simile = _____

37. SOL—isolate, soliloquy, solitary = _____

38. SOPH—philosopher, sophistication, sophomore = _____

39. SPEC—introspective, spectacle, spectator = _____

40. SUB—sublimate, submarine, subterranean = _____

41. TELE—telegraph, telephone, television = _____

42. TEN—tenacious, tenure, untenable = _____

43. THEOS—atheism, polytheistic, theology = _____

44. TRACT—extract, intractable, tractor = _____

45. TRANS—transcontinental, transfer, translate = _____

46. VAC—evacuate, vacation, vacuum = _____

47. VERT—convert, introvert, vertigo = _____

48. VIV—survivor, vivacious, vivid = _____

49. VOC—invoke, vocal, vociferous = _____

50. VOL—malevolent, volition, voluntary = _____

(Answers on page 269)

♦ A COMPOUND SUBJECT

Speakers and writers of English love to create new words by joining together two (or more) independent words to form compounds. You need only recall the parade of new compound words that marched into our language during the 1980s to realize how alive and well is the process of compounding. Among the compound creations of the last decade are *fast track, greenmail, insider trading, hostile takeover, power lunch, compact disc, computer virus, telephone tag, spreadsheet, user-friendly, designer jeans, ghetto blaster, safe sex, cold fusion, nuclear winter, breakdancing, baby boomer, exit poll, freebase, high five, bag lady, single parent, designated driver, wishlist,* and *couch potato.*

To compound your knowledge of how compound words work, try the triple-play game that follows. For the first section, examine the three words in each list and think of a word that could come before each of the three to form a compound, as in *black* bird, board, smith:

1. _____ hunter, line, quarters
2. _____ board, note, ring
3. _____ grenade, out, writing
4. _____ line, pass, product
5. _____ country, roads, word
6. _____ lands, school, way
7. _____ ball, locker, print
8. _____ book, key, port
9. _____ hat, liner, nosed

10. _____ hog, map, race
11. _____ cut, net, line
12. _____ bank, brother, feud
13. _____ bread, changed, hand
14. _____ draw, hold, stand
15. _____ bow, check, drop
16. _____ boat, letter, seat
17. _____ run, stretch, town
18. _____ card, lift, mask
19. _____ breaker, mill, shear
20. _____ job, plow, shoe

Now consider the three words in each list that follows and think of a word that could come after each one to form a compound, as in back, first, short *hand:*

21. bank, cook, text _____
22. bull's, evil, private _____
23. curtain, lightning, ram _____
24. board, cake, side _____
25. high, lime, moon _____
26. back, fore, under _____
27. left, pop, turn _____
28. every, no, some _____
29. base, foot, odd _____
30. love, steam, tug _____
31. back, eye, whip _____
32. hoe, show, touch _____
33. back, over, sounding _____

34. by, cross, pass _____

35. by, over, under _____

36. hind, in, over _____

37. down, water, wind _____

38. magic, no, talk _____

39. hand, machine, shot _____

40. big, hot, pot _____

Finally, supply the word that completes the compound begun by the first word and starts the compound completed by the second word, as in gentle *man* hole:

41. foot _____ point

42. front _____ backer

43. cook _____ case

44. space _____ mate

45. skeleton _____ note

46. tooth _____ ax

47. cow _____ scout

48. sweet _____ brush

49. open _____ tight

50. red _____ dog

(Answers on page 269)

♦ ## SPOT THAT ALLUSION

A front-page story in a St. Louis newspaper reported an incident in which two men were hospitalized after a fistfight. What had happened was that the driver of an automobile stopped for a red light at a main intersection. A man on the sidewalk called out, "Hey, mister, your left front tire is going flat." The driver got out, looked at the tire, and called to his benefactor, "Thanks for being a Good Samaritan!" Whereupon the pedestrian leapt off the curb and started pounding the driver with his fists, shouting, "You can't call me a dirty name!" The shocked driver struck back, and the result was that both men ended up in the hospital—all because one of them thought that a Samaritan was a dirty word.

Few of us will end up eating a knuckle sandwich because we miss the source of a literary allusion—in this case, Luke 10:30–37. But our lives are considerably enriched when we are able to spot such sources because allusions play an important role in creating impressions and emotions. Allusions allow us to experience an idea on two levels at once by linking what we are reading or hearing with what we have read or heard in the past. By enhancing the present through associations with experiences that glow through time, allusions become keys that unlock the doors to many mansions (itself a biblical reference to John 14:2, where Jesus says, "In my Father's house are many mansions.").

The richest source of present-day allusions is literature, especially the Bible, classical mythology, and Shakespeare. The lines that follow were all written during the

1980s, and each makes reference to a literary source. As specifically as you can, identify the source of each allusion and explain its use:

1. "Somebody had to suffer the slings and arrows and backhands of Martina Navratilova and Chris Evert-Lloyd while Wimbledon marks time until Martina and Chris get their hands on each other tomorrow."

2. "The Kaufmans say that the medical community forces them into a catch-22 situation. If they make significant progress with a child, doctors question whether the child was autistic. If no change occurs, doctors reject them as failures."

3. "The Giants, like Sisyphus's boulder, have dashed the hopes of their faithful and, at times, fanatical fans for all but two of the last 19 years."

4. "Such soaring rates of inflation are so new that a retiree would have needed the foresight of a Cassandra to prepare for the consequences."

5. "The basic problem with *A Second Chance* has little to do with the authors' data, presentation, or optimistic vision of a New Hampshire energy future without Seabrook. It is that Seabrook exists, rather like Bertha in the attic in *Jane Eyre*.

6. Title of a magazine story about Ferdinand Marcos: "Out, Damned Despot."

7. "At the same time, a variety of baby-girl dolls were born like Athena from the head of Zeus—or the head of the toy corporation."

8. From a story during the short-lived baseball strike of 1985: "[Peter] Uberroth hangs over these negotiations like the ghost of Banquo."

9. "For many Americans April is indeed the cruelest month because it contains April 15, the deadline for filing tax returns with the Internal Revenue Service."

10. "A 1983 Philadelphia 76ers championship banner proclaimed, 'Moses Parts the Lakers.' "

11. " 'In the last four years we've created six million new jobs!' cries the Great Communicator, and the rabble hiss and clap their chopped hands and throw up their sweaty nightcaps."

12. "There's no question for whom the bell tolls in Chile. It tolls for General Augusto Pinochet and for the dictatorship that has run Chile since 1973."

13. Title of a magazine article on contaminated fruit: "Do You Dare to Eat a Peach?"

14. "So why will Henniker reject such revenue? Because opponents of the landfill have made a clear, strong case that this gift is in reality a Trojan horse."

15. "Jesse Jackson declared that the party needed new wineskins to hold new wine."

16. From a story about a hapless New Jersey Devils hockey goalie: "He stoppeth one of three."

17. Hockey superstar Wayne Gretzky is often referred to as "The Great Gretzky."

18. In one installment of the comic strip "Peanuts," Lucy holds a football for the gullible Charlie Brown to kick. She quotes: "To everything there is a season, Charlie Brown . . . a time to be born and a time to die, a time to plant and a time to pluck up that which is planted." As Charlie runs at the football, Lucy, at just the right moment, snatches the ball away, causing Charlie to flip over and crash. Lucy stares at the fallen Charles and adds, "And a time to pull away the football."

19. "*Sunday Morning* comes into our living rooms on little cat's feet."

20. "For the next six months, Walesa guided that union across lines that no one dared dream possible in Eastern Europe. Visions of independence danced in Polish heads."

(Answers on page 269)

♦ FORMULAIC THINKING

The questions that follow look like a series of mathematical or scientific formulas, but they aren't. Instead, each formula represents a basic fact or a popular saying. This challenge does not measure your intelligence, and it is certainly not a measure of your mathematical abilities. But it is a test of one kind of creative and flexible thinking.

In taking this kind of test, most people solve fewer than half the problems on their first try, but they find that insights into additional answers come to them in sudden flashes when they return to the task a second or third time. Thus, you should answer all the questions you can and then stop. Later, come back to the quiz and try again. Only when you are sure that you have reached your limit should you consult the answers.

Now for the instructions. Each formula contains the initials of the words that make it intelligible. Identify the missing words. As examples, 7 D = 1 W is "seven days equal one week" and 26 L in the A is "twenty-six letters in the alphabet." When you have solved more than half the problems, you will gave gone A + B the C of D, that is to say, "above and beyond the call of duty":

1. 3 F = 1 Y
2. A + E + I + O + U = V
3. 50 S = USA
4. S + S + M + T + W + T + F = D of the W
5. M + NH + V + M + RI + C = NE

6. S + H of R = USC

7. "A P S = A P E"

8. 24 H = 1 D

9. N + P + V + A + A + P + C + 1 = the P O S

10. M + M + J + L = the 4 E

11. 4 K + 4 Q + 4 J = the FC

12. 8 P or 4 Q = 1 G

13. 12 M = 1 Y

14. F F = 100 Y

15. 18 H = a GC

16. "1 B in the H = 2 in the B"

17. D + H + G + S + B + S + D = the 7 D

18. 54 C in a D (with J)

19. 1000 C = 1 M

20. 26 M + 385 Y = 1 M

21. "1 S in T S 9"

22. 60 M = 1 H

23. 32 D F = the T at which W F

24. 64 S on a CB

25. HH + MH at 12 = N or M

26. A + E were in the G of E

27. C + 6 D = N Y E

28. "R = R = R"

29. AL + JG + WM + JFK = A P

30. 26 A in the C

31. 13 S + 50 S on the AF

32. 360 D = the C of a C

33. the N + the P + the SM = C S

34. "I B E except A C"

35. "N P = N G"

36. 16 O = 1 P

37. P + B + K + R + K + Q = C P

38. 40 D + 40 N = the G F

39. a 4 LC = GL

40. B or G − F + M = O
41. 10 D = 1 C
42. "N N = G N"
43. 12 I = 1 F
44. 9 P = the S S
45. 5,280 F = 1 M
46. P + A + A = the 3 M
47. "1 P = 1000 W"
48. "3 B M (S H T R)"
49. B + R + Y = the P C
50. 90 D = R A

(Answers on page 271)

◆ LETTER PERFECT

Language is very old, but writing is quite new. Humankind has been speaking for at least half a million years, but we have known how to write for fewer than six thousand, since the invention of cuneiform writing in Mesopotamia and hieroglyphic writing in ancient Egypt. Without writing we must depend upon the archeologist to glimpse what human life was like; with writing history begins.

Historical linguists generally agree that the earliest phonetic alphabet, in which written symbols stand for sounds rather than for objects or ideas, appears in inscriptions found near Mount Sinai, dating from around the fifteenth century B.C. This early Semitic alphabet, adopted by the Greeks, gave rise to the Roman alphabet, from which our system of writing stems.

The Greeks modified the names of the Semitic letters to conform with their own language. *Aleph* became *alpha,* *beth* turned into *beta, gimel* into *gamma, daleth* into *delta,* and so on. Our word *alphabet* is compounded of the first two Greek letters—alpha and beta.

Here's a game that asks you to take a fresh look at the letters in our alphabet. What do the letters in each cluster (which in each case have been alphabetized) have in common? For the first section, what aspect of sound unites the letters of each list?:

1. BCDEGPTVZ
2. AJK
3. FLMNSX

4. AEFHILMNORS
5. ABCDEFGHIJKLMNOPQRSTUVXYZ
6. ABCGIJOPQRTUY
7. BMPW

How the letters look accounts for the unity to be found in each of the following lists:

8. AEFHIKLMNTVWXYZ
9. abcdefghjmnopqrstu
10. ij
11. QX
12. ABDOPQR
13. abdegopq
14. jpqy
15. bdh
16. CGMNOPSUWXYZ
17. abcdeghlmnopqrsuvwz
18. AHIMOTUVWXY
19. BCDEHIKOX
20. HIOSXZ

Finally, what concept other than sound and letter-formation unites each of the following groupings?:

21. BCDFGHJKLMNPQRSTVXZ
22. CDILMVX
23. AJKQ
24. ABCDEFGHIJKLMNOPRSTUVWXY
25. EIOPQRTUWY

(Answers on page 273)

♦ PICTURESQUE WORDS

A rebus is a representation of words or phrases through pictures or letters whose names and relationships, when sounded out, yield the intended answer. Because they are a kind of visual pun, rebus puzzles have become very popular in our television age, in which the eyes have it.

I invite you to discover how harmoniously your eyes and brain can work together by translating a collection of picture puzzles into words or phrases. As a warm-up exercise, decide what well-known phrases are represented by the following three rebuses:

MAN   ‾‾‾‾‾‾‾‾
BOARD   READING   AALLLL
               ‾‾‾‾‾‾‾‾

The answers are "man overboard," "reading between the lines," and "all in all." Now that you are becoming an expert in traversing the rebus strip, have fun interpreting some more eye- and brainteasers:

1. Each of these rebuses relates to food:

MAY   KNEE   ME ME ME   GEGS
AAA   A LOT OF   AL AL AL

2. Each of these rebuses forms a common phrase:

MIND	STEP	PAID	DEATH/LIFE	ONE OTHER
MATTER	IT	I'M		ONE OTHER
		WORKED	SSA	ONE OTHER
				ONE OTHER
SP EE CH	poFISHnd	SUGAR		ONE OTHER
		Please		ONE OTHER

DOTHEPE   TIASTITCHME   HE/HIMSELF   HOU SE

ALL/world   LA BOR   PÓSITIVE   COF FEE   SHAVE

BUSTED

3. In each of these picture puzzles that which is lost can be found:

DANCER   PIT   WORL   SYMPHO   MORNING

4. A single verbal key unlocks each of these rebuses to reveal three related words:

DICE DICE   KEET KEET   M.D. M.D.

5. Come on up to these vertical rebuses:

T	H	GROUND	E	E	0	I I	C
O	A	FEET	M	L	M.D.	OO	O
W	N	FEET	A	K	Ph.D.		N
N	D	FEET	R	C	D.D.S.		
	S	FEET	F	U			
		FEET		B			
		FEET					

topless dancer

6. For the rebus expert, each of these configurations is one word:

M
E

FM

ABCDEFGHIJKMN
OPQRSTUVWXYZ

7. Finally, a rebus miscellany:

SAND	GAINS	LE VEL	222DAY	ECNALG

WEAR   KNEE   T   M CE M CE M CE
LONG   LIGHT   O
TORTILLA   HIJKLMNO

(Answers on page 274)

♦ ANSWERS

___

GOTCHA!

(page 241)

1. Neither. The sum of nine and seven is sixteen.

2. Twelve

3. Bread

4. The doctor is the boy's mother.

5. None. Peacocks don't lay eggs; peahens do.

6. Of course. July 4th occurs between July 3rd and July 5th.

7. Each man was playing a different opponent.

8. Nine

9. When the two buses are passing each other, both will be the same distance from Boston.

10. The rungs will never be underwater because the ship rises with the tide.

11. Mount Everest

12. No one can be sure, but something like "goo-goo" or "glug-glug."

13. Nine

14. Once. After that, the number is 20.

15. There is no dirt in a hole.

16. If a man has a widow, he is likely to be quite dead.

17. The last word is pronounced "masheenery," not "Mac-Hinery."

18. One

19. Nobody said that the other end of the leash was tied to anything.

20. One is not a nickel; it's a quarter. The other coin is a nickel.

21. Four. Because there are only three errors in the sentence, the word *five* becomes the fourth mistake.

22. Five. Most people get only three.

23. Survivors aren't buried anywhere.

24. They are two members of a set of triplets.

25. Neither. The capital of Pennsylvania is Harrisburg.

26. 40 degrees. A rock can't fall through ice.

27. Twenty-eight tries. After the twenty-seventh, the frog will reach the top with its next hop of three feet.

28. Six—five sisters and one brother (the speaker)

29. After fifty-five minutes

30. Because "You are the engineer," the age of the engineer is your age.

FIGURING OUT AUNT MATILDA

(page 245)

MY AUNT MATILDA LIKES: 1. words that contain double vowels **2.** words that are spelled correctly **3.** compound words **4.** words that contain internal rhyme **5.** plaindromic words—spelled the same forwards and backwards **6.** reversagram words, which spell a different word when read backwards **7.** homophones, which sound just like another word with a different spelling **8.** words in which only one vowel appears repeatedly **9.** words that begin and end with the same letter **10.** words that start with syllables that name parts of the body **11.** words with long vowels **12.** words that spell different words when the final *s* is moved to the front

DIG DOWN TO THE ROOTS

(page 248)

1. leader, ruler **2.** man, mankind **3.** self **4.** life
5. head **6.** time **7.** rule **8.** believe **9.** blame **10.** good
11. faith **12.** kind, species **13.** write **14.** heavy, weigh
15. flock, herd **16.** water **17.** law **18.** light, rise **19.** speak
20. large
21. bad **22.** send **23.** new **24.** all **25.** word, name
26. straight, correct **27.** all, entire **28.** foot **29.** push
30. love
31. many **32.** carry **33.** first **34.** feel **35.** follow
36. like **37.** alone **38.** wise, wisdom **39.** see, look
40. under
41. far away **42.** hold **43.** God **44.** pull **45.** across
46. empty **47.** turn **48.** life, lively **49.** call, voice **50.** wish

A COMPOUND SUBJECT

(page 252)

1. head **2.** key **3.** hand **4.** by **5.** cross **6.** high
7. foot **8.** pass **9.** hard **10.** road
11. hair **12.** blood **13.** short **14.** with **15.** rain
16. love **17.** home **18.** face **19.** wind **20.** snow
21. book **22.** eye **23.** rod **24.** walk **25.** light
26. ground **27.** over **28.** one or body **29.** ball **30.** boat
31. lash **32.** down **33.** board **34.** word
35. pass or play **36.** sight **37.** fall **38.** show **39.** gun
40. shot
41. ball **42.** line **43.** book **44.** ship **45.** key **46.** pick
47. boy or girl **48.** tooth **49.** air **50.** hot

SPOT THAT ALLUSION

(page 255)

1. In his famous soliloquy in *Hamlet,* Act III, Scene 1, Hamlet asks, "Whether 'tis nobler in the mind to suffer/The slings and arrows of outrageous fortune,/Or to take arms against a sea of troubles."

2. The title Joseph Heller's *Catch-22* refers to a military regulation that keeps pilots flying insanely suicidal missions. "Catch-22," now meaning "a problematic situation whose very nature denies any rational solution," has become the most frequently employed allusion in all of American literature.

3. In classical mythology Sisyphus is condemned to eternal punishment in the underworld, where he rolls a huge rock up a cliff, only to have it roll down again as he reaches the top. Now you know who was the first rock and roller.

4. Cassandra, daughter of the Trojan king, Priam, possessed an extraordinary ability to foretell the future, although no one would heed her warnings.

5. The Seabrook nuclear power plant in New Hampshire, like the mad Bertha Mason in Charlotte Brontë's *Jane Eyre,* simply will not disappear. Ultimately, Bertha sets fire to the house in which she is imprisoned and is consumed in the conflagration.

6. A punning reference to *Macbeth,* Act V, Scene 1. During her bouts of sleepwalking, Lady Macbeth imagines blood on her hands and exclaims, "Out, damned spot."

7. Athena, daughter of Zeus, sprang fully armed from her father's head.

8. In *Macbeth,* Act III, Scene 4, the ghost of the murdered Banquo appears at the Macbeths' banquet and ruins what might otherwise have been the social event of the year.

9. As the first line of T. S. Eliot's poem *The Waste Land* informs us, "April is the cruelest month."

10. In Exodus 14:1–31, Moses parted the waters of the Red Sea, and the Israelites passed through safely while the Egyptians pursuing them were drowned. On the banner, Moses refers to center Moses Malone and the Lakers to the Los Angeles Lakers.

11. In *Julius Caesar,* Act 1, Scene 2, Casca reports on the offering of the crown to Caesar: "And still as he refused it, the rabblement hooted and clapped their chopped hands and threw up their sweaty night-caps."

12. The title of Ernest Hemingway's novel *For Whom the Bell Tolls* hearkens back to a sermon by John Donne: "Any man's death diminishes me because I am involved in mankind, and therefore never send to know for whom the bell tolls; it tolls for thee."

13. In T. S. Eliot's "The Love Song of J. Alfred Prufrock," the wimpy speaker endlessly worries about whether he should "dare to eat a peach." After all, a peach has all that juice in it and a hard pit at its center.

14. In classical mythology, the Greeks sent a huge wooden horse as a gift to the Trojans, but inside were hiding a host of soldiers, who emerged by night and overthrew Troy.

15. In Matthew 5:17, Jesus advises, "Neither do men put new wine into old bottles: else the bottles break, and the wine runneth out, and the bottles perish: but they put new wine into new bottles, and both are preserved."

16. A brilliant reference to Samuel Taylor Coleridge's "The Rime of the Ancient Mariner." The mariner "stoppeth one in three" to tell his story of crime and punishment over and over again.

17. Gretzky's epithet is an allusion to F. Scott Fitzgerald's glittering hero, "the Great Gatsby."

18. In Ecclesiastes 3:1–8 we read: "To everything there is a season, and a time to every purpose under the heaven: A time to be born, and a time to die; a time to plant, and a time to pluck up that which is planted. . . ."

19. Carl Sandburg's "Fog" opens with "The fog comes/on little cat feet."

20. From Clement Clarke Moore's "The Night Before Christmas": "While visions of sugar plums danced in their heads."

FORMULAIC THINKING

(page 258)

1. three feet are one yard **2.** *a, e, i, o,* and *u* are the vowels **3.** 50 states make up the U.S. **4.** Saturday, Sunday, Monday, Tuesday, Wednesday, Thursday, and Friday are the days of the week

5. Maine, New Hampshire, Vermont, Massachusetts, Rhode Island, and Connecticut make up New England   **6.** The Senate and the House of Representatives make up the U.S. Congress   **7.** "A penny saved is a penny earned."   **8.** 24 hours in a day   **9.** noun, pronoun, verb, adjective, adverb, preposition, conjunction, and interjection are the parts of speech   **10.** Matthew, Mark, Luke, and John are the four evangelists

11. four kings, four queens, and four jacks are the face cards   **12.** eight pints or four quarts equal a gallon   **13.** twelve months equal one year   **14.** a football field is one hundred yards   **15.** eighteen holes in a golf course   **16.** "A bird in the hand is worth two in the bush."   **17.** Doc, Happy, Grumpy, Sneezy, Bashful, Sleepy, and Dopey are the Seven Dwarves   **18.** fifty-four cards in a deck (with jokers)   **19.** a thousand centuries are a millennium   **20.** twenty-six miles and 385 yards equal a marathon

21. "A stitch in time saves nine."   **22.** sixty minutes equal one hour   **23.** 32 degrees Fahrenheit is the temperature at which water freezes   **24.** sixty-four squares on a chess or checker board   **25.** hour hand and minute hand at twelve is noon or midnight   **26.** Adam and Eve were in the Garden of Eden   **27.** Christmas plus six days is New Year's Eve   **28.** "A rose is a rose is a rose."   **29.** Abraham Lincoln, James Garfield, William McKinley, and John Fitzgerald Kennedy were assassinated presidents   **30.** twenty-six amendments in the Constitution

31. thirteen stripes and fifty stars on the American flag   **32.** 360 degrees in the circumference of a circle   **33.** the *Nina, Pinta,* and *Santa Maria* were Columbus's ships   **34.** *i* before *e* except after *c*   **35.** "No pain, no gain."   **36.** sixteen ounces make a pound   **37.** pawn, bishop, knight, rook, king, and queen are the chess pieces   **38.** forty days and forty nights were the Great Flood   **39.** a four-leaf clover is good luck   **40.** a boy or a girl without a father and mother is an orphan

41. ten decades is a century   **42.** "No news is good news."   **43.** twelve inches is a foot   **44.** nine planets in the solar system   **45.** 5,280 feet make a mile   **46.** Porthos, Aramis, and Athos are the Three Musketeers **47.** "A picture is worth a thousand words." **48.** "Three blind mice (see how they run)." **49.** blue, red, and yellow are the primary colors **50.** ninety degrees make a right angle

LETTER PERFECT

(page 261)

1. All letters rhyme, ending with an *ee* sound.

2. All letters rhyme, ending with an *ay* sound.

3. All letters begin with an *eh*.

4. All letters begin with vowel sounds. That is each would be preceded by the article *an*.

5. One syllable. Amazingly, the single letter *W* generates three syllables.

6. Each letter sounds the same as a full word: *a, bee, see/sea, gee, eye/I, jay, oh, pea/pee, queue/cue, are, tea/tee, you/ewe/yew, why*. I could have added K (*quay*), L (*el*), M (*em*), N (*en*), and X (*ex*), but these seldom-used words might have confused you.

7. Each letter is pronounced by putting the lips together.

8. Made with straight lines

9. Made with curved lines

10. Dotted letters. The only lowercase word in English with three consecutive dotted letters is the variant spelling *hijinks*.

11. Letters with a line crossing over

12. and 13. Letters enclosing an open area

14. Lowercase descenders

15. Lowercase ascenders

16. and 17. Letters normally printed without lifting pen from paper. Some might add B, D, and R.

18. Vertical symmetry: the left and right sides of each letter are mirror images. Hence, these letters will appear the same when they are held up to a mirror.

19. Horizontal symmetry: the top and bottom of each letter are mirror images.

20. Each letter remains the same when turned upside down.
21. Consonants, excluding *Y* (as in *rhythm*) and *W* (as in *cwm*).
22. Roman numerals
23. Letters appearing on playing cards
24. Letters on a telephone dial
25. First row of letters on a standard *qwerty* keyboard.

PICTURESQUE WORDS

(page 263)

1. mayonnaise, a lot of baloney, three square meals, scrambled eggs

2. mind over matter, step on it, I'm overworked and underpaid, life after death, ass backwards, six of one and a half dozen of the other, parts of speech, big fish in a small pond, pretty please with sugar on top, the inside dope, a stitch in time, he's beside himself, a house divided, it's a small world after all, division of labor, accentuate the positive, coffee break, close shave, flat busted

3. topless dancer, bottomless pit, world without end, unfinished symphony, top of the morning

4. paradise, parakeets, paradox (pair of docs)

5. downtown, hands down, six feet underground, frameup, buckle up, three degrees below zero, circles under the eyes, condescending

6. asinine, anemone, effeminacy, noel (no *l*)

7. sandbox, capital gains, split level, Tuesday, backward glance, long underwear, neon light, lean-to, high chair, three blind mice (no *i*'s), Tortilla Flat, water (H to O = H_2O)